WISDOM

from

T.D. JAKES

WISDOM

from

T.D.
JAKES

T.D. Jakes

Compiled by Angela Rickabaugh Shears

DESTINY IMAGE® PUBLISHERS, INC.
P.O. Box 310, Shippensburg, PA 17257-0310

"Speaking to the Purposes of God for This Generation and for the Generations to Come."

This book and all other Destiny Image, Revival Press, MercyPlace, Fresh Bread, Destiny Image Fiction, and Treasure House books are available at Christian bookstores and distributors worldwide.

For a U.S. bookstore nearest you, call **1-800-722-6774.**

For more information on foreign distributors, call **717-532-3040.**

Reach us on the Internet: **www.destinyimage.com.**

Hardcover: Trade Paper:
ISBN 10: 0-7684-3151-4   ISBN 10: 0-7684-3202-2
ISBN 13: 978-0-7684-3151-3   ISBN 13: 978-0-7684-3202-2
Media Gift Set ISBN 13: 978-0-7684-4221-2

For Worldwide Distribution, Printed in the U.S.A.

Hardcover: 1 2 3 4 5 6 7 8 9 10 11 / 13 12 11 10
Trade Paper: 1 2 3 4 5 6 7 8 9 10 11 / 13 12 11 10

Contents

INTRODUCTION

Wisdom

SOLOMON asked God for it. Universities espouse its virtues. Pastors pray for it. Parents want to believe their children have it. Students hope for it. Executives bank on it. Some rationalize it. Others brag about it. Most want more of it.

Dietrich Bonhoeffer, who stood firm against Hitler's policies during World War II and was subsequently executed for his stance, defines wisdom this way, "To understand reality is not the same as to know about outward events. It is to perceive the essential nature of things. The best-informed man is not necessarily the wisest. Indeed there is a danger that precisely in the multiplicity of his knowledge he will lose sight of what is essential. But on the other hand, knowledge of an apparently trivial detail quite often makes it possible to see into the depth of things. And so the wise man will seek to acquire the best possible knowledge about events, but always without becoming dependent upon this knowledge. To recognize the significant in the factual is wisdom."

Within today's 24-7 communication culture, it is many times hard to "recognize the significant in the factual." In our virtual reality worldwide society, someone's "wisdom" can be— and is—blogged, Twittered, Skyped, emailed, and Facebooked instantaneously to others next door or in a faraway continent. Allowing wisdom to become relative is opening doors for imposters to barge in. Only with God's wisdom can believers forge ahead to make the world a safer, stronger, and more beautiful place.

How much better to get wisdom than gold! And to get understanding is to be chosen rather than silver (Proverbs 16:16 NKJV).

God's wisdom, shared through His committed and dedicated servants, has carried people through ages past full of danger, through current economic and worldwide unrest, and will continue to protect and defend His children throughout eternity. Only wisdom from Heaven provides peace that passes all human understanding.

Wisdom From T.D. Jakes is a compilation of bits of wisdom received from the Lord over many years of serving Him. Shared with you are 40 wise and personal insights to refresh and empower you to tackle life's challenges, rejoice in God's promises fulfilled, and shout victory over the enemy.

This interactive devotional journal immerses you into a world where God's powerful wisdom infuses you as never before. You will gain the strength to solve problems, turn situations around, and learn how to make wise decisions.

"I believe there are times when we grow weary of human answers. The crucial times that arise in our lives require more than good advice. We need a word from God." –T.D. Jakes

Within each chapter are wise reflections from best-selling books along with provocative "Points to Ponder" that help you delve into the depths of yourself to search out things, issues, people, situations, and just plain stuff that you need to deal with to be able to move forward toward your God-given destiny.

"Words of Wisdom" from other well-known believers will make you laugh, cry, and become a more thinking Christian as you consider other points of view about important topics. A place for your own special thoughts is provided to record your heart's desires, feelings, ideas, wonderings, and inner yearnings.

This treasured keepsake launches you onto a road filled with wisdom and paved with God's glory.

1

Wisdom and Peace

We are enveloped in peace when we know that nothing the enemy does can abort the plan of God for our lives. Greater still is the peace that comes from knowing we cannot rush God's timing. When the Lord speaks a word into our lives, it is like a seed. It takes time for a seed to sprout. God knows when we have reached the time of germination. Our confidence is in God's seed.

(Excerpts from *Can You Stand to be Blessed?*)

Wisdom and Peace Reflections

WHEN the promise has grown in the fertile ground of a faith-filled heart and reached the time of maturation, it will come to pass. It will be a direct result of the presence of God. It will not be by human might or power, but by the Spirit of the Lord (see Zech. 4:6). The psalmist David said, *"My times are in Thy hand"* (Ps. 31:15a). For me there is a sense of tranquility that comes from resting in the Lord. His appointment for us is predetermined. There is a peace that comes from knowing God has included us in His plan—even the details.

I can remember as a very small child following close behind my mother, an educator in the public school system. She was often asked to speak at luncheons and banquets. Her sorority attracted the kind of successful ladies who had achieved academic and sociological accomplishments. These were the kind of ladies who extended their pinky fingers when they drank tea from china cups and saucers. These matronly madams of the 1960s prided themselves on being classy and distinguished. After the festivities had subsided and we were traveling from what I remember to be a rather stuffy atmosphere, I said to my mother, "Today, I travel with you and listen while you speak, but the time will come when you will travel with me and I will speak!" What was strange was this prophetic utterance came from the mouth of a then-devilish little six-year-old who, though very precocious, was nevertheless an ordinary child who would one day have a supernatural encounter with God!

I don't know how at that early age that I knew I had an appointment with destiny, but I somehow sensed that God had a purpose for my life. I earnestly believe that everyone is pre-destined to accomplish certain things for the Lord. Somewhere in the recesses of your mind there should be an inner know-ing that directs you toward an expected end. For me, it is this awareness that enables me to push myself up out of the bed and keep fighting for survival. You must be the kind of tenacious person who can speak to the enemy and tell him, "My life can't end without certain things coming to pass. It's not over until God says, 'It's over!'"

Points to Ponder

Nothing the enemy does
can abort the plan of God for your life.

You cannot rush God's timing.

When the Lord speaks a word into your life, it is like a seed.

Is your confidence in God's seed?

God has included you in His plan—even the details.

Do you sense God's purpose for your life?

Words of Wisdom

*And let the **peace** of God rule in your hearts, to which also you were called in one body; and be thankful* (Colossians 3:15 NKJV).

Peace begins with a smile.

–Mother Teresa

*Grace, mercy, and **peace** will be with you from God the Father and from the Lord Jesus Christ, the Son of the Father, in truth and love* (2 John 1:3 NKJV).

While in London, I took the opportunity to steal away to an old cemetery. I noticed that almost all the tombstones, including a child's, had the words "Rest in Peace" inscribed on them.

I wondered: *How can you rest in peace if you died with all your potential inside?*

Immediately a quiet voice screamed in my head: *Is it not a greater tragedy if those who lived to old age also carried their books, art, music, inventions, dreams, and potential to the grave?*

You have been endued with natural talents, gifts, desires, and dreams. All humanity, in all cultures, races, and socio-economic situations, lives with the natural instinct to manifest their potential.

–*Myles Munroe Devotional & Journal*[1]

My Wisdom Keys

_____

_____

_____

_____

_____

_____

_____

_____

_____

_____

_____

2

Wisdom in Knowing God

Because the world did not receive Him, did not see Him, and did not know Him, the Lord of glory was crucified.

Only Christ's inner circle of Peter, James, and John witnessed His transfiguration (see Matt. 17:1-9). Only these three saw the inner turmoil of Jesus as He poured out His soul in prayer and conformed to the Father's will in the Garden of Gethsemane (see Matt. 26:37-44).

Only John went to the cross. Is it any wonder that he received an amazing vision known as "The Revelation of Jesus Christ"? Before receiving this vision, he was exiled to the isle of Patmos.

(Excerpts from *Anointing Fall on Me*)

Wisdom in Knowing God Reflection

JESUS spoke mysteries to His beloved friend John that still perplex the world—and even the Church. In order to receive this surpassing revelation, John had to detach himself from earthly things. He heard a voice say, *"Come up hither, and I will shew thee things which must be hereafter"* (Rev. 4:1).

God calls those who are committed to excellence to a place of seclusion and aloneness. The Holy Ghost is saying, "Detach yourself from things that blind you from seeing My mysteries and deafen you from hearing My language."

Jesus is speaking, but even those in the Church are missing Him because they do not hear His language. Many are not hearing His voice because tradition has left them content with only the first glimpse of His glory. The glory of Christ far exceeds any glory ever known by man. In those three short years Jesus began to reveal the mysteries of a powerful Kingdom that was greater than any problem, sickness, or dilemma.

Why did the people crucify the Prince of Glory? Jesus Christ had a message, power, and authority that frightened the religious hierarchy of His day. Yes, He was a Jew who spoke the regional dialect. But sometimes He also spoke mysteries to His disciples. Thousands followed Christ, but He handpicked 12 to be with Him.

Why aren't more believers hearing from God? Many are not walking in obedience and do not have the fullness of the Holy Ghost. Jesus only reveals His secrets to those who are trustworthy and have intimate fellowship with Him.

Jesus told His disciples that the world would not understand, see, or know, but those who had the Holy Ghost would.

Yet a little while, and the world seeth me no more; but ye see me: because I live, ye shall live also. At that day ye shall know that I am in my Father, and ye in me, and I in you (John 14:19-20).

He was saying, "In that day they will see me as dead, but you will know that I am still in control. When they bury Me in a tomb, some will say it's over. But you will know I spoke mysteries the world could not understand. 'Destroy this temple and in three days I will raise it up." When they come on that first Easter morning and find My body gone, they will say it was stolen. You will know that I have risen from the dead. My ministry will continue through the Holy Ghost."

Points to Ponder

Jesus speaks mysteries to His beloved friends.

God calls those who are committed to excellence.

Why did the people crucify the Prince of Glory?

He has handpicked you to be with Him.

Why aren't more believers hearing from God?

Jesus reveals secrets to those who have
intimate fellowship with Him.

Words of Wisdom

Know God, know peace. No God, no peace.

–Popular bumper sticker

( )

Jesus spoke these words, lifted up His eyes to heaven, and said: "Father, the hour has come. Glorify Your Son, that Your Son also may glorify You, as You have given Him authority over all flesh, that He should give eternal life to as many as You have given Him. And this is eternal life, that they may know You, the only true God, and Jesus Christ whom You have sent (John 17:1-3 NKJV).

( )

"Our seeking must be sincere and we should always be ready to make a deeper commitment. When that is the case, God will move and send His Holy Spirit to touch each of us in a special way."[1]

( )

*I will give you the treasures of darkness and hidden riches of secret places, that you may **know** that I, the Lord, who call you by your name, am the God of Israel* (Isaiah 45:3 NKJV).

( )

These people are the ones who will experience the Manifest Presence of God—God's Presence manifesting itself in healing and restoration, in power and protection, and intimacy and friendship.

–Don Nori Sr., Manifest Presence[2]

MY WISDOM KEYS

_____

_____

_____

_____

_____

_____

_____

_____

_____

_____

_____

_____

_____

3

Wisdom in Hearing God

God is definitely speaking to His people. The question is: Can we hear Him? The Holy Ghost is speaking right now. He is speaking words of truth and guidance. He speaks what He hears in Heaven.

Whenever the Holy Ghost speaks, He testifies that He has been in the boardroom of Heaven. Hearing from Him causes us to lift our head. Just when satan thought he had you, to his amazement you begin to shout. He doesn't know it, but you heard a word.

(Excerpts from *Anointing Fall on Me*)

Wisdom in Hearing God Reflection

YOU may be going through a valley, but the Holy Ghost told you that Jesus is the Lily of the Valley. You may be going down a perplexing path, but you heard that Jesus is a Wonderful Counselor. You may be going through a famine in your life and ministry, but you heard a word that said, "Trust Me when you can't trace Me." You may be facing an insurmountable trial, but you heard a word that said, "Stand still and see the salvation of the Lord."

I heard a word, and you can, too. Sometimes the word is for you, and sometimes it is for someone else. Sometimes God merely wants to use you as a spokesperson.

Jonah's name means carrier pigeon. God had a message for him to deliver to a third party, the people of Nineveh. Allow God to use you in the same way.

Has someone ever tried to relay a message to you over the phone? The words they spoke weren't their own, but belonged to someone else. Someone gave them a message, and they, in turn, repeated what they heard.

In the same way, the Holy Ghost has you on the line and speaks a word to you. It may not be a word directly from the Bible, but it is a *rhema* word designed to fit your crisis. Remember that the Holy Ghost doesn't speak on His own initiative. He doesn't convey His own ideas or plans. He speaks only what He hears from Heaven.

Let's look at seven areas of your life in which the Holy Ghost wants to speak. The Holy Ghost:

1. Wants to speak to you things that go beyond human logic, natural tendency, and physical comprehension.

2. Will testify to you.

3. Will give you direction.

4. Speaks to lead us to obedience (see Acts 10:1-23).

5. Shows you God's choice for companionship.

6. Will speak and close doors that were the right thing but the wrong time.

7. Sometimes warns us.

Points to Ponder

Is Jesus your Lily of the Valley?

Are you allowing God to use you?

He will lead you in the right direction.

Have you heard Him?

The Holy Ghost speaks only what He hears from Heaven.

Are you listening for God's voice?

Words of Wisdom

You may call me crazy, my own family and friends may call me crazy, and I may even call myself crazy at times. But crazy as it may be, when I hear God, it's the most exhilarating rush I've ever had in my life.

–Kim Clement, *Call Me Crazy, But I'm Hearing God*[1]

...faith comes from hearing the message, and the message is heard through the word of Christ. But I ask: Did they not hear? Of course they did: "Their voice has gone out into all the earth, their words to the ends of the world" (Romans 10:17-18 NIV).

Next I heard the audible voice of God. He told me to return to my wife and daughter. My wife, Joy, had become an agnostic when she was exposed to atheistic professors in college. But when I showed her the predictions about the Jewish people written thousands of years in advance in the Bible, she said, 'I must believe the Bible is from God.' She became a believer in Jesus shortly thereafter.

–Sid Roth, *They Thought for Themselves*[2]

There are two kinds of people: those who say to God, 'Thy will be done,' and those to whom God says, "All right, then, have it your way".

–C. S. Lewis

Unfortunately, many in the Church miss the great blessing of fellowship with our Lord because we have lost the ability to recognize His voice within us. Though we have the promise that 'My sheep hear My voice,' too many believers are starved for that intimate relationship that alone can satisfy the desire of their hearts. I was one of those sheep who was deaf to his Shepherd until the Lord revealed four very simple keys (found in Habakkuk 2:1-2) that unlocked the treasure of His voice.

–Mark Virkler[3]

MY WISDOM KEYS

4

Wisdom in Building Up

In the following passage we find some of the simplest and most profound truths in all the Word of God. But everything hinges on the truth stated in verse 20:

> **But ye, beloved, building up yourselves on your most holy faith, praying in the Holy Ghost,** *keep yourselves in the love of God, looking for the mercy of our Lord Jesus Christ unto eternal life. And of some have compassion, making a difference: and others save with fear, pulling them out of the fire; hating even the garment spotted by the flesh* (Jude 20-23).

(Excerpts from *Release Your Anointing*)

Wisdom in Building Up Reflections

E can build up ourselves, cultivate a sense of expectancy about the coming of the Lord, have compassion on those who have fallen, and be moved with zeal to make a difference in the lives of those who have spotted their garments.

Let's look at the ability to "build up." The word *build* is an architectural word that means "to cause a building to stand." It means "to lay a good foundation." In the natural realm, it is always important to leave yourself the ability to add on to your building in case you need to expand in the future. If you have outgrown your spiritual house, the Holy Ghost gives you the resources to add on to meet your demands.

If you have more ministry, then you have a place to house it, to build on. Are there weak areas in the structure? Build them up. You do this by praying in the Holy Spirit. This will build up your faith so that you can stand against Goliath and know that your God is bigger than the giant who defies you.

God sent Elijah to a widow in *Zarephath*, which means "to refine as in a melting pot." Gold is not pure in its original form. It must be refined, which is done by heating it to boiling. The heat separates the raw substance from its impurities which surface and are skimmed off. God does the same for us using the heat of trials to separate the gold from the dross in our lives.

God leads you through a progressive path, but the ultimate goal is to be on Mount Carmel and to be fruitful. He wants you to be able to call fire down from Heaven, to see into the Spirit as Elijah saw, and to persevere in prayer until God intervenes in your situation. The answer to your drought may appear to be a cloud the size of a man's hand, but you know a refreshing rain is about to fall.

If you feel a hunger to go on with God, the Holy Ghost is telling you that your current spiritual house is too small. He is urging you to build on your current foundation. In order to do this, however, we must pray in the Holy Ghost.

Points to Ponder

Are you building up your spiritual life?

Stand strong against giants who come against you.

God is leading you to be fruitful.

God wants you to be able to call fire down from Heaven.

Persevere in prayer until God answers.

Is the Holy Ghost telling you that your current
spiritual house is too small?

Words of Wisdom

He is like a man building a house, who dug deep and laid the foundation on the rock. And when the flood arose, the stream beat vehemently against that house, and could not shake it, for it was founded on the rock. (Luke 6:48 NKJV)

To live in courage requires encouragement. And sometimes the only one to encourage you is you. Not knowing how to strengthen ourselves has cost the Church dearly. It is the key to promotion! It is what turned David's darkest hour into the backdoor to the throne room. And it will be the same for you. When you learn how to strengthen yourself, you will reach your destiny, fulfill your God-born dreams, and become a person who can accurately represent Jesus—re-resenting Jesus to the world.

–Bill Johnson, *Strengthen Yourself in the Lord*[1]

*So it is with you. Since you are eager to have spiritual gifts, try to excel in gifts that **build up** the church* (1 Corinthians 14:12 NIV).

You can actually think yourself into and out of situations. You can make yourself ill with your thoughts and by the same token you can make yourself well by the use of a different and healing type of thought. Think positively, for example, and you set in motion positive forces which bring positive results to pass.

–Norman Vincent Peale, *The Power of Positive Thinking*[2]

MY WISDOM KEYS

5

Wisdom and Purpose

You would be surprised to know how many people there are who never focus on a goal. They do several things haphazardly without examining how forceful they can be when they totally commit themselves to a cause. The difference between the masterful and the mediocre is often a focused effort. On the other hand, mediocrity is masterful to persons of limited resources and abilities. So in reality, true success is relative to ability. What is a miraculous occurrence for one person can be nothing of consequence to another. A person's goal must be set on the basis of his ability to cultivate talents and his agility in provoking a change.

(Excerpts from *Hope for Every Moment*)

Wisdom and Purpose Reflections

I am convinced that I have not fully developed my giftings. I am committed to being all that I was intended and predestined to be for the Lord, for my family, and for myself. How about you—have you decided to roll up your sleeves and go to work? Remember, effort is the bridge between mediocrity and masterful accomplishment!

If you are only talented, you may feel comfortable taking your talents into a secular arena. Talent, like justice, is blind; it will seek all opportunities the same. But when you are cognizant of divine purpose, there are some things you will not do because they would defeat the purpose of God in your life! Being called according to purpose enables you to focus on the development of your talent as it relates to your purpose!

Within our decaying shells, we constantly peel away, by faith, the lusts and jealousies that adorn the walls of our hearts. If the angels were to stroll through the earth with the Creator and ask, "Which house is Yours?" He would pass by all the mansions and cathedrals, all the temples and castles. Unashamedly, He would point at you and me and say, "That house is Mine!"

Yes, it is true: Despite all our washing and painting, this old house is still falling apart! We train it and teach it. We desperately try to convince it to at least think differently. But like a squeaky hinge on a swollen door, the results of our efforts, at best, come slowly. The Holy Ghost Himself resides beneath this sagging roof.

God Himself has—of His own free will and predetermined purpose—put us in the embarrassing situation of entertaining a Guest whose lofty stature so far exceeds us that we hardly know how to serve Him!

Whenever we bring our efforts into alignment with His purpose, we automatically are blessed. Our efforts must be tailored after the pattern of divine purpose. Everyone is already blessed. We often spend hours in prayer trying to convince God that He should bless what we are trying to accomplish. What we need to do is spend hours in prayer for God to reveal His purpose. When we do what God has ordained to be done, we are blessed because God's plan is already blessed.

Points to Ponder

Have you fully developed your giftings?

Are you committed to being all that you were intended and predestined to be for the Lord, for my family, and for yourself?

Effort is the bridge between mediocrity and masterful accomplishment!

When your efforts are in alignment with His purpose, you will be blessed.

Your efforts must be tailored after the pattern of His divine purpose.

Words of Wisdom

Who hath saved us, and called us with an holy calling, not according to our works, but according to His own purpose and grace, which was given us in Christ Jesus before the world began (2 Timothy 1:9).

⟨ ⟩

The purpose of your life is far greater than your own personal fulfillment, your peace of mind, or even your happiness. It's far greater than your family, your career, or even your wildest dreams or ambitions. If you want to know why you were placed on this planet, you must begin with God.

–Rick Warren, *The Purpose Driven Life*[1]

⟨ ⟩

Many people have a wrong idea of what constitutes true happiness. It is not attained through self-gratification, but through fidelity to a worthy purpose.

–Helen Keller

⟨ ⟩

A hundred million angels accompany me as I journey through the years of my life. It's a distinctive joy to the angels when each of God's children follows their urging to visit the heavenly realm in our human state. There, in the heavenly realm, *I meet with and walk with* the Lord Jesus. I experience the glory and purpose of God, the Father, beyond my finite understanding.

–Marie Chapian, *Angels in Our Lives*[2]

⟨ ⟩

Can you define the focus, intent, purpose, and drive of your heart? Is Christ at the center of your world? Do you talk to Him daily?

Does He talk to you about what you're supposed to do, who you're supposed to look like and where you're supposed to have your focus? It's got to be Christ. Meeting Jesus changes a person. You can't stay the same.

–Bob Lenz, *Grace*[3]

MY WISDOM KEYS

6

Wisdom and Significance

There is a deep-seated need in all of us to sense purpose—even out of calamity. Out of this thirst for meaning is born the simplistic yet crucial prayer, *'Why?'*....

(Excerpts from *Hope for Every Moment*)

Wisdom and Significance Reflections

NO matter how painful the quest, we will still search through the rubbish of broken dreams, broken promises, and twisted childhood issues looking for clues. We don't have to necessarily erase the cause of our pain; we mainly just want to find some reason or justification for the pain and discomfort.

All of us know what it means to be left alone. Whether through death, desertion, or even disagreement, we have all been left alone at times. We are sometimes disillusioned when we find out how easily people will leave us. Generally they leave us when we think that we need them.

The struggle truly begins not when men surround us, but rather when they forsake us. It is then that we begin to discover our own identity and self-worth!

In whom also we have obtained an inheritance, being predestinated according to the purpose of Him who worketh all things after the counsel of His own will (Ephesians 1:11).

Have you reached that place in life where you enjoy your own company? Have you taken the time to enjoy your own personhood? When other people give affirmation, it reflects their opinion about you. When they leave, you may feel worthless and insignificant. But when you speak comfort and blessings to yourself, it reflects your own opinion about yourself. The best scenario is to enjoy both kinds of affirmation.

There are reasons to give yourself a standing ovation. The first is the fact that your steps are carefully observed and arranged by God Himself. They are designed to achieve a special purpose in your life. The Bible says, *"If God be for us, who can be against us?"* (Rom. 8:31b). So you must rejoice because you are in step with the beat of Heaven and the purposes of God. Second, you ought to rejoice because you are pursuing a goal that defies human manipulation. Your blessing rests in accomplishing the will of God.

Points to Ponder

Are you still searching through the rubbish of broken
dreams, broken promises, and twisted childhood
issues looking for clues of your pain?

Discover your own identity and self-worth
after people have forsaken you.

Have you reached that place in life where
you enjoy your own company?

Have you taken the time to enjoy your own personhood?

Speak comfort and blessings to yourself—it reflects
your own opinion about yourself.

Your blessing rests in accomplishing the will of God.

Words of Wisdom

I knew that I had a special calling, yet even though God had spoken some things to me and had made some promises, for a while it didn't look like I was moving in that direction. But God was working in my life all the time. I can see now that it was all part of my training.

–Faisal Malick, *Positioned to Bless*[1]

For the Scripture says to Pharaoh: "I raised you up for this very purpose, that I might display My power in you and that My name might be proclaimed in all the earth" (Romans 9:17 NIV).

Now, storms and hits will come in life, but just because you have some challenges doesn't mean you're not in the will of God. I've rejoiced in that thought many times in my life, and particularly during the most recent altercation when I was punched in the eye during an altar call.

–Billy Joe Daugherty, *Knocked Down, But Not Out*[2]

We can change the world.

–Dr. D. James Kennedy

MY WISDOM KEYS

_____

_____

_____

_____

_____

_____

_____

_____

_____

_____

_____

_____

_____

7

Wisdom of Fire

God places His prize possessions in the fire. The precious vessels that He draws the most brilliant glory from often are exposed to the melting pot of distress. The bad news is, even those who live godly lives will suffer persecution. The good news is, you might be in the fire, but God controls the thermostat! He knows how hot it needs to be to accomplish His purpose in your life. I don't know anyone I would rather trust with the thermostat than the God of all grace.

(Excerpts from *Hope for Every Moment*)

Wisdom of Fire Reflections

EVERY test has degrees. Some people have experienced similar distresses, but to varying degrees. God knows the temperature that will burn away the impurities from His purpose. He has had to fan the flames to produce the effects that He wanted in my life. God is serious about producing the change in us that will glorify Him.

His hand has fanned the flames that were needed to teach patience, prayer, and many other invaluable lessons. We need His corrections. We don't enjoy them, but we need them. He affirms our position in Him by correcting and chastening us.

Yea doubtless, and I count all things but loss for the excellency of the knowledge of Christ Jesus my Lord: for whom I have suffered the loss of all things, and do count them but dung, that I may win Christ...that I may know Him... (Philippians 3:8-10).

There are times in our lives when God will take us from one realm of faith to another. Christ knows what kind of heat to place upon us to produce the faith needed in the situation. When we present our bodies as living sacrifices, He is the God who answers by fire. The good news lies in the fact that when our faith collapses beneath the weight of unbelievable circumstances, He gives us His faith to continue on....

As the fire of persecution forces us to make deeper levels of commitment, our faith needs to be renewed to match our level of commitment. There is a place in God where the fire consumes every other desire but to know the Lord in the power of His resurrection. All other pursuits tarnish and seem worthless in comparison. Perhaps this is what Paul really pressed toward, that place of total surrender.

Points to Ponder

God is serious about producing the change in
you that will glorify Him.

You need His corrections.

He gives you His faith to continue.

Your faith needs to be renewed to match
your level of commitment.

There is a place in God where the fire
consumes every other desire.

Are you pressing toward that place of total surrender?

Words of Wisdom

A mother may cry profusely after hearing that her only son has to serve a mandatory ten-year sentence for drug trafficking. Another mother facing the same situation with her son may look at imprisonment as a blessing from God, knowing that now her child is safer than if he were on the streets. It all depends on how you look at it.

–Noel Jones, *God's Gonna Make You Laugh*[1]

I indeed baptize you with water unto repentance. but He that cometh after me is mightier than I, whose shoes I am not worthy to bear: He shall baptize you with the Holy Ghost, and with fire (Matthew 3:11).

We feel free when we escape—even if it be but from the frying pan to the fire.

–Eric Hoffer

Each one's work will become clear; for the Day will declare it, because it will be revealed by fire; and the fire will test each one's work, of what sort it is. If anyone's work which he has built on it endures, he will receive a reward (1 Corinthians 3:13-14 NKJV).

Shall I seek glory, then, as vain men seek, oft not deserved? I seek not mine, but His Who sent me, and thereby witness whence I am.

–John Milton, *Paradise Regained*

MY WISDOM KEYS

_____

_____

_____

_____

_____

_____

_____

_____

_____

_____

_____

_____

8

Wisdom Through Healing

I believe it is important that women get healed and released in their spirits. I believe that God will move freshly in the lives of women in an even greater way. God knows how to take a mess and turn it into a miracle. If you're in a mess, don't be too upset about it because God specializes in fixing messes. God is saying some definite things about women being set free and delivered to fulfill their purpose in the Kingdom.

(Excerpts from *Hope for Every Moment*)

Wisdom Through Healing Reflections

WHEN the Lord gets through working on you, all your adversaries will be ashamed. The people who contributed to your sense of low self-esteem will be ashamed when God gets through unleashing you. You won't have to prove anything. God will prove it. He will do it in your life. When He gets through showing that you've done the right thing and come to the right place, they will drop their heads and be ashamed.

If you have a past that torments you, Jesus can set you free. He will unleash your potential.

> *But I am poor and needy; yet the Lord thinketh upon me: Thou art my help and my deliverer; make no tarrying, O my God* (Psalm 40:17).

Can you imagine how hard life was for the infirm woman who was bowed over? (See Luke 13.) She had to struggle, because of her problem, to come to Jesus. Few of us are crippled in the same way. However, we all face crippling limitations. We can be bowed over financially. We can be bowed over emotionally. We can be bowed over where we have no self-esteem. He wants to see us struggling toward Him. Jesus could have walked to this woman, but He chose not to. He wants to see us struggle toward Him.

He wants you to want Him enough to overcome obstacles and to push in His direction. He doesn't want to just throw things at you that you don't have a real conviction to receive. When you see a humped-over person crawling through the crowd, know that that person really wants help. That kind of desire is what it takes to change your life. Jesus is the answer. It doesn't matter what the problem is, He is the answer.

Points to Ponder

God specializes in fixing messes.

Are you bowed over?

Jesus can set you free and unleash your potential.

Are you struggling toward Him?

Struggling toward Him will change your life.

Jesus is the answer.

Words of Wisdom

Unlike our panicky prayers, he quietly and calmly said, 'I command the spirit of death to leave and the life of God to flow into you now in the name of Jesus.' And as quickly as she had arched her back, she slowly and quietly laid back on the cot, her blue fingernails turning a pale pink. She was going to be all right.

–Flo Ellers, *Activating the Angelic*[1]

Grace is given to heal the spiritually sick, not to decorate spiritual heroes.

–Martin Luther

He healeth the broken in heart, and bindeth up their wounds (Psalm 147:3).

Friends had already begun to console him [John G. Lake] over her impending death. But Lake suddenly came to a realization that all sickness—not just some—was from the enemy. He then telegraphed a number of friends, telling them that his wife would be healed at 9:30 A.M. the next morning. That morning, he laid hands on her himself and she instantly recovered.

–John Crowder, *The New Mystics*[2]

MY WISDOM KEYS

9

Wisdom of Progressing

Many individuals in the Body of Christ are persevering without progressing. They wrestle with areas that have been conformed to the world instead of transformed. This is particularly true of us Pentecostals who often emphasize the gifts of the Spirit and exciting services. It is imperative that, while we keep our mode of expression, we understand that transformation doesn't come from inspiration! Transformation takes place in the mind.

(Excerpts from *Hope for Every Moment*)

Wisdom of Progressing Reflections

THE Bible teaches that we are to be renewed by the transforming of our minds (see Rom. 12:2; Eph. 4:23). Only the Holy Spirit knows how to renew the mind. The struggle we have inside us is with our self-perception. Generally, our self-perception is affected by those around us. Our early opinion of ourselves is deeply affected by the opinions of the authoritative figures in our formative years. If our parents tend to neglect or ignore us, it tears at our self-worth. Eventually, though, we mature to the degree where we can walk in the light of our own self-image, without it being diluted by the contributions of others.

> *For we are His workmanship, created in Christ Jesus unto good works, which God hath before ordained that we should walk in them* (Ephesians 2:10).

Jesus knew who He was. The Lord wants to help you realize who you are and what you are graced to do. To ask someone to define you without first knowing the answer yourself is dangerous. When you understand that He is the only One who really knows you, then you pursue Him with fierceness and determination. Pursue Him!

God knows who we are and how we are to attain our calling. This knowledge, locked up in the counsel of God's omniscience, is the basis of our pursuit, and it is the release of that knowledge that brings immediate transformation. He knows the hope or the goal of our calling. He is not far removed from us; He reveals Himself to people who seek Him. The finders are the seekers. The door is opened only to the knockers and the gifts are given to the askers! (See Luke 11:9.) Initiation is our responsibility. Whosoever hungers and thirsts shall be filled. Remember, in every crisis He is never far from the seeker!

Points to Ponder

Transformation doesn't come from inspiration!

Transformation takes place in your mind.

Do you have a healthy self-perception?

Do you realize who you are and what you are graced to do?

He reveals Himself to people who seek Him.

Initiation is your responsibility.

Words of Wisdom

And be not conformed to this world: but be ye transformed by the renewing of your mind, that ye may prove what is that good, and acceptable, and perfect, will of God (Romans 12:2).

It is this infilling that permits living water to flow and results in joy beyond human understanding. He wants us to be filled with joyous passion because without it, it will be impossible to leave the wilderness and cross our Jordan River.

–Israel Kim, *Find Your Promised Land*[1]

Moving me down the highway, rolling me down the highway, moving ahead so life won't pass me by.

–Jim Croce, "I've Got a Name"

I like the dreams of the future better than the history of the past.

–Thomas Jefferson

MY WISDOM KEYS

_____

_____

_____

_____

_____

_____

_____

_____

_____

_____

_____

10

Wisdom in Switching Channels

Sometimes we need to speak in our natural language according to our heritage. Sometimes, however, our natural language is no match for the warring spirits between earth and the throne of God.

When prayers in our natural language are being intercepted and shot down, Paul tells us to switch channels.

(Excerpts from *Anointing Fall on Me*)

Wisdom in Switching Channels Reflections

ALLOW the Holy Ghost within you to speak out on earth what Heaven is speaking into your spirit. This is praying in tongues, or praying in the Spirit.

Satan does not understand the language of Heaven. God's ways, which are so much higher than our ways, include praying in tongues. This leaves satan confused as to how to attack us. He may assign an evil spirit to attack our prayer life and report back to him so he can make a counterattack. But when we pray in the Spirit, or pray in tongues, we frustrate his plans.

Speaking in tongues places a great arsenal of spiritual weaponry at your disposal. Not knowing this, however, many believers struggle in prayer and intercession.

Likewise the Spirit also helpeth our infirmities: for we know not what we should pray for as we ought: but the Spirit itself maketh intercession for us with groanings which cannot be uttered. And he that searcheth the hearts knoweth what is the mind of the Spirit, because he maketh intercession for the saints according to the will of God (Romans 8:26-27).

Romans 8:26 contains a word that is often overlooked, and that is the very first word, *likewise.* The word means "in like manner, or to be similar to."

We cannot understand the language of God in our own intellect. I like to explain it like this: When a child who cannot talk plainly wants something, he or she may be able to speak only portions of words. A stranger may not understand, but the child's mother can make out the language. Even though the baby talk is barely intelligible, she understands the need. Taking a bunch of stammering, broken remarks, she interprets the language to meet the need.

Sometimes in order to get what you need from God, you must go from one language (our human intellect) to another language (the Holy Ghost).

Points to Ponder

Sometimes your natural language is no match for the warring spirits between earth and the throne of God.

Satan does not understand the language of Heaven.

When you pray in the Spirit, or pray in tongues, you frustrate satan's plans.

Speaking in tongues places a great arsenal of spiritual weaponry at your disposal.

You cannot understand the language of God in your own intellect.

God understands your need.

Words of Wisdom

If you are having a trial, or are tempted to fall into sin in some area of your life, seek help from the Holy Spirit. The Holy Spirit will help you overcome the problem. Pray in the Spirit and He will help you.

–Frank Bailey, *Holy Spirit, The Promised One*[1]

For we know that the whole creation groaneth and travaileth in pain together until now. And not only they, but ourselves also, which have the firstfruits of the Spirit, even we ourselves groan within ourselves, waiting for the adoption, to wit, the redemption of our body (Romans 8:22-23).

The gifts and anointing, spiritual acuity, and all of our spiritual senses will become more sensitive to the realm of the Spirit. As we begin to exercise our spiritual gifts and operate with greater sensitivity, the Lord releases us to touch people at a deeper level and see them set free from afflictions and bondages.

–Bruce Allen, *Promise of the Third Day*[2]

The passionate, sometimes rhythmic, language-like patter that pours forth from religious people who "speak in tongues" reflects a state of mental possession, many of them say. Now they have some neuroscience to back them up.

–Benedict Carey, *New York Times*[3]

MY WISDOM KEYS

11

Wisdom of Pentecost

Before He ascended into Heaven, Jesus commanded His disciples to tarry for the promise of the Holy Ghost.

Behold, I send the promise of my Father upon you: but tarry ye in the city of Jerusalem, until ye be endued with power from on high (Luke 24:49).

They had to wait only because the Holy Ghost was making His debut. Now that He has come, however, those who experience a Passover by accepting Jesus Christ, God's Passover Lamb, can receive the baptism of the Holy Ghost.

(Excerpts from *Anointing Fall on Me*)

Wisdom of Pentecost Reflections

MANY people have not received the Holy Ghost because they feel unworthy. If your own worthiness were the issue, you wouldn't have anything from God. The Christian life is founded on grace from beginning to end.

God does not see you as you are, but He sees you through the blood of Jesus. When Jesus died on the cross, you died with Him. God reckons you to be dead with Christ. *Reckon* means to figure in something, to write it down, to document it, to take inventory. Although you did not die physically, document your death with Christ because God sees you in Him when He died.

That's why you must have a Passover before you can have a Pentecost. Passover makes you worthy and a fit candidate for Pentecost. Passover applies the blood to the doors of your heart. The two side posts and top lintel of a doorway form a cross, which is a type of our coming through the cross of Jesus.

Gaining proper standing with God always requires the death of a substitute. God shed the blood of an innocent animal and clothed Adam and Eve with its skins after the fall (see Gen. 3:21). Each Israelite household in Egypt killed an innocent lamb to mark their doors with its blood (see Exod. 12:3-7). Years later it took the blood of a sinless, innocent man to atone for sin.

Every area of your life has been put under the blood of Jesus. He has become your *atonement*, which means a covering, to put away or to cancel. It also means to reconcile and to make at one with.

God says you are worthy to receive the baptism of the Holy Ghost. Jesus has prayed for you to receive the Comforter. Is it based on your merit? Of course not. You never have and never will live up to the expectations of a holy God. Jesus, Who *"ever liveth to make intercession"* (Heb. 7:25), prays confidently because He died in your stead.

Points to Ponder

Jesus commanded His disciples to tarry for the
promise of the Holy Ghost.

God sees you through the blood of Jesus.

You must have a Passover before you can have a Pentecost.

Every area of your life has been put under the blood of Jesus.

God says you are worthy to receive the baptism
of the Holy Ghost.

Jesus died in your stead.

Words of Wisdom

When the day of Pentecost came, they were all together in one place. Suddenly a sound like the blowing of a violent wind came from heaven and filled the whole house where they were sitting. They saw what seemed to be tongues of fire that separated and came to rest on each of them (Acts 2:1-3 NIV).

The Lord wants to use you to touch others' lives for eternity. People in your family will be changed when you are filled with the Holy Spirit. It won't be through your natural ability, but by Christ who is at work in you through the Holy Spirit.

–Larry Kreider and Dennis De Grasse, *Supernatural Living*[1]

There is a difference between the gift of tongues for the purpose of interpretation and our prayer language. We all have the ability to pray in tongues. When we do, we are speaking to God and not to man.

–Frank Bailey, *Holy Spirit, The Promised One*[2]

By declaring that Pentecost was a fulfillment of Joel's prophecy, Peter was officially stating that the Last Days had begun. This passage [Acts 2:17-18] implies that the language of dreams, visions, and prophecy by which He will speak to His people will bridge generational barriers, crash through the gender gap, and cross all social boundaries.

–Kris Vallotton, *Developing a Supernatural Lifestyle*[3]

MY WISDOM KEYS

12

Wisdom and His Army

Without a word from God, without the energizing breath of the Holy Ghost, you are only a mere form of what you can be. This is similar to the valley of dry bones that Ezekiel saw. Before the prophet lay a potential army, but without the Word of the Lord they were merely a form of what they could have been.

(Excerpts from *Anointing Fall on Me*)

Wisdom and His Army Reflections

ET'S look at some principles we can learn from Ezekiel 37:

1. You must be willing to confess your condition. *"They were very dry"* (vs. 2).

2. You must confess that you are merely a form of what you could be.

    - The valley was *"full of bones"* (vs. 1).

    - The structure of an army was just waiting for God's command.

3. You must hear the Word of God. *"Prophesy upon these dry bones, and say unto them, O ye dry bones, hear the word of the Lord"* (vs. 4).

    - The anointing only falls upon truth. God will not put His seal of approval on something until He is sure that it is His.

    - The Word brings the truth that ultimately sets us free (John 8:32).

4. The Word will bring about change.

    - The dry bones heard their potential. *"I will cause breath to enter into you, and ye shall live"* (vs. 5).

    - They knew they were not complete at this stage. *"I will*

lay sinews upon you, and will bring flesh upon you, and cover you with skin" (vs. 6). The Word brought about a noise as broken pieces began to come together (vs. 7). God will speak to your broken and shattered dreams.

- The Word formed real people with arms, legs, eyes, and feet. They were still not complete, however. *"But there was no breath in them"* (vs. 8).

5. The potential was realized as the word brought about the wind. *"Prophesy unto the wind, prophesy, son of man, and say to the wind, Thus saith the Lord God; Come from the four winds, O breath, and breathe upon these slain, that they may live"* (vs. 9).

- The wind gave potential, the ability to carry out what they were capable of doing. The Word came from the four corners of the earth. There isn't an area that God cannot fill with the Holy Ghost. Your past, your childhood, your feelings of inferiority, your wounds, your loneliness. The Holy Ghost can fill all of you.

- No matter what others say, God sees incredible potential in you. The Word of God says you're capable. Within you is an army. You merely need the wind to breathe on that which God has formed in you.

Points to Ponder

The structure of an army was just waiting
for God's command.

God will not put His seal of approval on something
until He is sure that it is His.

God can fill your past, your childhood, your feelings of
inferiority, your wounds, your loneliness.

God sees incredible potential in you.

The Word of God says you are capable.

Within you is an army.

Words of Wisdom

To reach for your full potential, focus on your areas of competence, have the courage to take action despite obstacles, and strive to improve continually by passionately pursuing a vision of excellence.

–Kris Den Besten, *Shine: Five Empowering Principles for a Rewarding Life*[1]

( )

The Lord gives voice before His army, for His camp is very great; for strong is the One who executes His word. For the day of the Lord is great (Joel 2:11 NKJV).

( )

The hidden world of the spirit is the only true eternal world. Everything in this present world is passing away, but the hidden realm of the spirit lasts forever. For this reason alone, entrance into the hidden realm of the spirit is literally a life and death matter.

–Mark Van Deman, *A Traveler's Guide to the Spirit Realm*[2]

( )

Suddenly I saw a white horse march forth. On the stirrup leather down the side of its saddle was written the word 'Holiness.' Then I saw another word, 'Holy War.' At the same time I saw the Lord as a warrior stepping forward and mounting His war horse.

–James W. Goll and Lou Engle, *The Call of the Elijah Revolution*[3]

MY WISDOM KEYS

13

Wisdom in That Certain Place

What encourages me when I go through the storms of life? I look in the Word of God and find that someone else has already been there and made it through. We are surrounded by witnesses:

Wherefore seeing we also are compassed about with so great a cloud of witnesses, let us lay aside every weight, and the sin which doth so easily beset us, and let us run with patience the race that is set before us (Hebrews 12:1).

In each instance, however, these saints had to get to a certain place before they saw the manifestation of God.

(Excerpts from *Release Your Anointing*)

Wisdom in that Certain Place Reflections

NOAH endured a torrential downpour that flooded the earth for months, but he had a place that gave him access to God. On the third level of the ark a window gave him access to the heavenlies.

> *A window shalt thou make to the ark, and in a cubit shalt thou finish it above; and the door of the ark shalt thou set in the side thereof; with lower, second, and third stories shalt thou make it* (Genesis 6:16).

In the midst of his storm he found solace and peace.

Jacob struggled for years with who he was, compared to who he wanted to be. His wrestling climaxed when he got to Jabbok, which means to pour out, to empty. Jacob went alone to Jabbok, the place of struggle where he wrestled with an angel. Divinity met with humanity, and Jacob's thigh was put out of joint. Upon arriving at the place, the patriarch was Jacob (swindler, supplanter, cheater), but after the struggle, his name was Israel (prince of God). It was a place of power, as God gave him power with Himself and man (Gen. 32:21-29).

Moses struggled with his leadership responsibilities over the nation of Israel. The demands of the multitude taxed Moses to the point of exhaustion. Moses asked God for a manifestation of His glory. But before Moses could see this manifestation, he had to get to a certain place. Hidden in the cleft of a rock, Moses saw the afterglow of God's glory, but only after he got to that place.

If you're a believer in Christ, you have some type of calling on your life. You may be a pastor or a leader in the church. You may have a specific gift that needs to be stirred up. Like Jacob, you may be struggling with who you are.

In these last days, satan and all his cohorts are waging a final onslaught against the Church. We must know God in a way in which we have never known Him before. Within some of you are miracles, unborn babies, ministries, and gifts. We all have callings.

Because of circumstances—perhaps something beyond your control; perhaps because of your faults, failures, or your past life—satan has told you that your baby, your gift, your ministry, must be aborted. But satan is a liar. Scripture tells us *"the gifts and callings of God are without repentance"* (Rom. 11:29). You need to get to where you can see the raw, undiluted presence of God and His anointing. Only then can you release your anointing to bring glory to His Kingdom.

Points to Ponder

What encourages you when you go through
the storms of life?

As a believer, you have some type of calling on your life.

You may have a specific gift that needs to be stirred up.

Are you struggling with who you are?

Satan is a liar—don't listen to his lies.

Get to where you can see the raw, undiluted presence of
God and release your anointing.

Words of Wisdom

The Love Shack is the holiest place in the entire universe. It is a special place for only you and your Lord. Angels literally stand guard and prevent anything from entering that is contrary to God's purposes for you. This is the place where all that is evil, destructive, and hateful is excluded.

–Don Nori Sr., *The Love Shack*[1]

But God, who is rich in mercy, for his great love wherewith he loved us, even when we were dead in sins, hath quickened us together with Christ (by grace ye are saved), and hath raised us up together, and made us sit together in heavenly places in Christ Jesus (Ephesians 2:4-6).

Likewise, Jesus has conquered satan. And, spiritually speaking, He has taken us away and relocated us. We no longer live under satan's rule. We have been relocated into the Kingdom of Christ. Although physically we are still on planet Earth, spiritually we sit with Christ in heavenly places.

–Dr. Richard Booker, *Living in His Presence*[2]

A man can no more diminish God's glory by refusing to worship Him than a lunatic can put out the sun by scribbling the word, 'darkness' on the walls of his cell.

–C. S. Lewis

For Christ is not entered into the holy places made with hands, which are the figures of the true; but into heaven itself, now to appear in the presence of God for us (Hebrews 9:24).

MY WISDOM KEYS

_____

_____

_____

_____

_____

_____

_____

_____

_____

_____

_____

_____

14

Wisdom in Faith

Hebrews chapter 11 discusses at length the definition of faith. It then shares the *deeds* of faith in verses 32-35a, and finally, it discusses the *perseverance* of faith in verses 35b-39.

There are distinctions of faith as well. In Hebrews 11:32-35a, the teaching has placed an intensified kind of emphasis on the distinct faith that escapes peril and overcomes obstacles: *"Quenched the violence of fire, escaped the edge of the sword, out of weakness were made strong, waxed valiant in fight, turned to flight the armies of the aliens"* (Heb. 11:34).

(Excerpts from *Release Your Anointing*)

Wisdom in Faith Reflections

HOWEVER, in the verses that end the chapter [Hebrews 11], almost as if they were footnotes, the writer deals with the distinctions of another kind of faith. In his closing remarks, he shares that there were some other believers whose faith was exemplified *through* suffering and not *from* suffering.

And others had trial of cruel mockings and scourgings, yea, moreover of bonds and imprisonment: They were stoned, they were sawn asunder, were tempted, were slain with the sword: they wandered about in sheepskins and goatskins; being destitute, afflicted, tormented (Hebrews 11:36-37).

Christianity's foundation is not built on elite mansions, stocks and bonds, or sports cars and cruise-control living. All these things are wonderful if God chooses to bless you with them. However, to make finances the symbol of our faith is ridiculous. The Church is built on the backs of men and women who withstood discomfort for a cause. These people were not the end but the means whereby God was glorified. Some of them exhibited their faith through their shadows' healing sick people. Still others exhibited their faith by bleeding to death beneath piles of stone. They also had a brand of faith that seemed to ease the effect, though it didn't alter the cause.

As the fire of persecution forces us to make deeper levels of commitment, it is so important that our faith be renewed to match our level of commitment. There is a place in God where the fire consumes every other desire but to know the Lord in the power of His resurrection. At this level, all other pursuits tarnish and seem worthless in comparison. Perhaps this is what Paul really pressed toward, that place of total surrender. Certainly that is the place I reach toward, which often escapes my grasp, but never my view. Like a child standing on his toes, I reach after a place too high to be touched. My hands are extended, my feet are on fire—and I listen for His voice!

Points to Ponder

Some believers' faith was exemplified *through* suffering and not *from* suffering.

To make finances the symbol of your faith is ridiculous.

Your faith must be renewed to match your level of commitment.

Are you reaching toward that certain place in Him?

Are your hands extended and your feet on fire?

Are you listening for His voice?

Words of Wisdom

More fully, the fruit of Faith—in this aspect of trustfulness—may be defined as a quiet, steady, unwavering trust in the goodness, wisdom, and faithfulness of God. No matter what trials or seeming disasters may be encountered, the person who has cultivated this form of fruit remains calm and restful in the midst of the all.

–Derek Prince, *Faith to Live By*[1]

So then faith cometh by hearing, and hearing by the word of God (Romans 10:17).

One of the actions of faith is speaking. In fact, speaking is probably the primary action of faith. Every visible work of faith comes from speaking what needs to be manifested, healed, rebuked, or cast out into actual physical existence. We often talk about praying for the sick, but Jesus never did that. He just spoke and told the sicknesses and the demons to go, and they immediately went.

–Alan Vincent, *The Good Fight of Faith*[2]

A true faith in Jesus Christ will not suffer us to be idle. No, it is an active, lively, restless principle; it fills the heart, so that it cannot be easy till it is doing something for Jesus Christ.

–George Whitefield

MY WISDOM KEYS

15

Wisdom in Searching

Searching releases answers. The Word declares, *"Seek, and ye shall find"* (Matt. 7:7b). Many things available to us will not be found without an all-out search. Seeking God also takes focus. This search has to be what the police call an A.P.B. What does that mean? An *A.P.B.* is an "all points bulletin." The entire department is asked to seek the same thing. Thus, our search can't be a distracted, half-hearted curiosity. There must be something to produce a unified effort to seek God. Body, soul, and spirit—all points—seeking the same thing. There is a blessing waiting for us. It will require an A.P.B. to bring it into existence, but it will be worth attaining. Who knows what God will release if we go on an all-out God-hunt.

(Excerpts from *Release Your Anointing*)

Wisdom in Searching Reflections

I believe there are times when we grow weary of human answers. The crucial times that arise in our lives require more than good advice. We need a word from God. There are moments when we need total seclusion. We come home from work, take the telephone receiver off the hook, close the blinds, and lie before God for a closer connection. In Job's case, he was going through an absolute crisis. His finances were obliterated. His cattle, donkeys, and oxen were destroyed. His crops were gone. In those days it would be comparable to the crash of the stock market. It was as if Job, the richest man, had gone bankrupt. What a shock to his system to realize that all are vulnerable. It is sobering to realize that one incident, or a sequence of events, can radically alter our lifestyles.

Unfortunately, it generally takes devastation on a business level to make most men commit more of their interest in relationships. Job probably could have reached out to his children for comfort, but he had lost them, too. His marriage had deteriorated to the degree that Job said his wife abhorred his breath (see Job 19:17). Then he also became ill. Have you ever gone through a time in your life when you felt you had been jinxed? Everything that could go wrong, did! Frustration turns into alienation. So now what? Will you use this moment to seek God or to brood over your misfortune? With the right answer, you could turn the jail into a church!

Like a rainstorm that will not cease, the waters of discouragement begin to fill the tossing ship with water. Suddenly, you experience a sinking feeling. However, there is no way to sink a ship when you do not allow the waters from the outside to get on the inside! If the storms keep coming, the lightning continues to flash, and the thunder thumps on through the night, what matters is keeping the waters out of the inside. Keep that stuff out of your spirit!

Points to Ponder

Your search for God can't be a distracted,
half-hearted curiosity.

Your effort must be unified when seeking God.

One incident, or a sequence of events,
can radically alter your lifestyle.

Sometimes it takes devastation on a business level to make
most men commit more of their interest in relationships.

Will you use this moment to seek God or to
brood over your misfortune?

What matters is keeping the waters out of the inside.

Words of Wisdom

Seek ye the Lord while He may be found, call ye upon Him while He is near: let the wicked forsake his way, and the unrighteous man his thoughts: and let him return unto the Lord, and He will have mercy upon him; and to our God, for He will abundantly pardon (Isaiah 55:6-7).

Hungry people need to be fed or they will go search for what they need for themselves. It is true that shipwreck is often their end as they wander through the maze of religion and legalistic control.

–Don Nori Sr., *Secrets of the Most Holy Place Volume Two*[1]

The men who have done the most for God in this world have been early on their knees. He who fritters away the early morning, its opportunity and freshness, in other pursuits than seeking God will make poor headway seeking Him the rest of the day. If God is not first in our thoughts and efforts in the morning, He will be in the last place the remainder of the day.

–E. M. Bounds.

God made sure we could recognize the Messiah by giving us over 300 identifying marks, which were described by the prophets of Israel.

–Sid Roth, *The Incomplete Church*[2]

MY WISDOM KEYS

16

Wisdom in Praying in the Spirit

Praying in tongues helps you relieve anxiety. Jesus told His disciples, *"Come ye yourselves apart into a desert place, and rest a while"* (Mark 6:31).

Praying in the Spirit allows you to *come apart* before you come apart. Many of you are under severe pressure. You are tense, battle weary. Like the disciples, you need a solitary place to rest awhile.

(Excerpts from *Release Your Anointing*)

Wisdom in Praying in the Spirit Reflections

PRAYING in the Spirit pulls us into an experience with God and enables us to release our anointing. It's not surprising that Paul wondered whether he was in the body or out of the body. The apostle saw and heard things unlawful for a man to speak. God in the Spirit takes us to paradise, pulling us apart from the pressures of the world before we are pulled apart.

A piece of material does not come apart suddenly. It unravels bit by bit. If you don't repair it, a small tear can cause the whole garment to come apart. Praying in the Spirit brings us to that solitary place with God to help cope with stress, pressure, and anxiety. If your life is falling apart, your need is similar to the woman with the issue of blood. She wanted to touch the hem of Christ's garment. She realized the hem was where all loose ends were put back together. This is what praying in the Spirit will do.

The apostle Paul wrote, *"What is it then? I will pray with the spirit, and I will pray with the understanding also: I will sing with the spirit, and I will sing with the understanding also"* (1 Cor. 14:15). "I will pray with the spirit," means that you rely on the Holy Ghost to guide you as you pray. He will speak, but we must listen. When we pray with the Spirit, we are praying with the knowledge of God's will:

Likewise the Spirit also helpeth our infirmities: for we know not what we should pray for as we ought: but the Spirit itself maketh intercession for us with groanings which cannot be uttered (Romans 8:26).

When we pray in the Spirit, we pray with fervency and intensity as the Spirit gives us the unction to focus on what we are praying for and to diligently seek God.

Points to Ponder

Praying in tongues helps you relieve anxiety.

Praying in the Spirit allows you to *come apart* before you come apart.

God in the Spirit takes you to paradise.

Praying in the Spirit brings you to that solitary place with God to help cope with stress, pressure, and anxiety.

When you pray with the Spirit, you are praying with the knowledge of God's will.

When you pray in the Spirit, the Spirit gives you the unction to focus and to diligently seek God.

Words of Wisdom

Whenever you come before the Father in prayer, remember that by His Spirit in you, you have a divine link that enables you to commune and worship Him in the Spirit. You have been given divine access into the Holy of Holies and stand before Him in His awesome Presence.

–Morris Cerullo, *How to Pray*[1]

You must pray with all your might. That does not mean saying your prayers, or sitting gazing about in church or chapel with eyes wide open while someone else says them for you. It means fervent, effectual, untiring wrestling with God...This kind of prayer be sure the devil and the world and your own indolent, unbelieving nature will oppose. They will pour water on this flame.

–William Booth.

Praying always with all prayer and supplication in the Spirit, and watching thereunto with all perseverance and supplication for all saints; and for me, that utterance may be given unto me, that I may open my mouth boldly, to make known the mystery of the gospel (Ephesians 6:18-19).

My journey through the Bible that night turned out to be one of the most impactful experiences of my life. I began to reason, *If I'm going to pray in the Spirit, then I must be filled with the Spirit.*

–Neil T. Anderson, *Praying by the Power of the Spirit*[2]

My Wisdom Keys

_____

_____

_____

_____

_____

_____

_____

_____

_____

_____

_____

_____

17

Wisdom, Not Pity Parties

Jesus seldom attended funerals. When He did, it was to arrest death and stop the ceremony. If you are planning an elaborate ceremony to celebrate your nonparticipation in the plan of God, I must warn you that God doesn't hang around funerals. Sometimes Christians become frustrated and withdraw from activity on the basis of personal struggles. They think it's all over, but God says not so! The best is yet to come. The Lord doesn't like pity parties, and those who have them are shocked to find that although He is invited, He seldom attends. Many morbid mourners will come to sit with you as you weep over your dear departed dreams. But if you want the Lord to come, you mustn't tell Him that you aren't planning to get up.

(Excerpts from *Insights to Help You to Survive Peaks & Valleys*)

Wisdom, Not Pity Parties Reflections

IF you ever get around people who have accomplished much, they will tell you that those accomplishments didn't come without price. Generally that cost is much more expensive than you normally want to pay. Still, the cost of total transformation means different things to different people. When you arrive at your destination, don't be surprised that some people will assume everything you achieved came without price. The real price of success lies within the need to persevere. The trophy is never given to someone who does not complete the task. Setbacks are just setups for God to show what He is able to do. Funerals are for people who have accepted the thought that everything is over. Don't do that; instead tell the enemy, "I am not dead yet."

For a just man falleth seven times, and riseth up again: but the wicked shall fall into mischief (Proverbs 24:16).

The whole theme of Christianity is one of rising again. However, you can't rise until you fall. Now that doesn't mean you should fall into sin. It means you should allow the resurrecting power of the Holy Ghost to operate in your life regardless of whether you have fallen into sin, discouragement, apathy, or fear. There are obstacles that can trip you as you escalate toward productivity. But it doesn't matter what tripped you; it matters that you rise up. People who never experience these things generally are people who don't do anything. There is a certain safety in being dormant. I would rather walk on the water with Jesus. I would rather nearly drown and have to be saved than play it safe and never experience the miraculous.

When the AIDS epidemic hit this country, pandemonium erupted. Terror caused many people, Christians as well as non-Christians, to react out of ignorance and intimidation. The media continually presented the sickness as it attacked many individuals in highly visible positions. In listening to the discussions on TV and elsewhere, the primary concern didn't seem to be for the victim. People were whispering, wanting to know how it was contracted. I told the church I pastor that it was absolutely absurd to concern themselves with how anybody contracted AIDS. The issue is that they have it, and what are we going to do to help?

Points to Ponder

The best is yet to come.

The Lord doesn't like pity parties.

The cost of total transformation means different
things to different people.

Setbacks are just setups for God to show
what He is able to do.

I would rather walk on the water with Jesus.

What are you going to do to help?

Words of Wisdom

Four months later, I ran into Jennifer in the mall. With tears stream-
ing down her face, she introduced me to her adoptive mother and her
daughter, of whom she regained custody. Both of those relationships
have been restored, and Jennifer is pursuing her relationship with
God....

–Greg Holmes, *If He Builds It, They Will Come*[1]

*In the fear of the Lord is strong confidence: and his children shall have
a place of refuge* (Proverbs 14:26).

It is a peculiar sensation, this double-consciousness, this sense of
always looking at one's self through the eyes of others, of measuring
one's soul by the tape of a world that looks on in amused contempt
and pity.

–W. E. B. DuBois

Prolonged self-pity produces many problems for the sufferer as it
holds them a victim of their own circumstances. –Marion Meyers,
The ABC's of Emotions[2]

God uses the encouragement of the Scriptures, the hope of our ultimate salvation in glory, and the trials that He either sends or allows
to produce endurance and perseverance.

–Jerry Bridges, *The Practice of Godliness*[3]

My Wisdom Keys

18

Wisdom and Regret

A terrible thing happens to people who give up too easily. It is called *regret*. It is the nagging, gnawing feeling that says, "If I had tried harder, I could have succeeded." When counseling married couples, I always encourage them to be sure they have done everything within their power to build a successful marriage. It is terrible to lay down at night thinking, "I wonder what would have happened if I had tried this or that." Granted, we all experience some degree of failure. That is how we learn and grow. If a baby had to learn how to walk without falling, he would never learn. A baby learns as much from falling on his bottom as he does from his first wobbly steps.

(Excerpts from *Insights to Help You Survive Peaks & Valleys*)

Wisdom and Regret Reflections

YOU would be surprised to know how many people there are who never focus on a goal. They do several things haphazardly without examining how forceful they can be when they totally commit themselves to a cause. The difference between the masterful and the mediocre is often a focused effort. On the other hand, mediocrity is masterful to persons of limited resources and abilities. So in reality, true success is relative to ability. What is a miraculous occurrence for one person can be nothing of consequence to another. A person's goal must be set on the basis of his ability to cultivate talents and his agility in provoking a change. I often wonder how far my best work is in front of me. I am convinced that I have not fully developed my giftings. But, I am committed to the cause of being. "Being what?" you ask. I am committed to being all that I was intended and predestined to be for the Lord, for my family, and for myself. How about you—have you decided to roll up your sleeves and go to work? Remember, effort is the bridge between mediocrity and masterful accomplishment!

Multiple talents can also be a source of confusion. People who are effective at only one thing have little to decide. At this point, let me distinguish between talent and purpose. You may have within you a multiplicity of talent. But if the Holy Spirit gives no direction in that area, it will not be effective. Are you called to the area in which you feel talented? On the other hand, consider this verse: "And we know that all things work together for good to them that love God, to them who are the called according to His purpose" (Rom. 8:28). So then you are called according to His purpose and not your talents. You should have a sense of purpose in your ministry and not just talent.

Points to Ponder

A baby learns as much from falling on his bottom as he does from his first wobbly steps.

Are you focused on a goal?

True success is relative to ability.

Are you committed to being all that you are intended and predestined to be for the Lord, for your family, and for yourself?

Effort is the bridge between mediocrity and masterful accomplishment!

You are called according to His purpose and not just your talents.

Words of Wisdom

Some of them were ready to quit and go back to Egypt. Others just said, 'Forget it. If this is what God has planned for me, I don't want it.' In spite of their gross lack of faith, God performed a miracle there on the desert sands, turning bitter waters into sweet waters.

–Bill Wilson, *Christianity in the Crosshairs*[1]

( )

Godly sorrow brings repentance that leads to salvation and leaves no regret, but worldly sorrow brings death (2 Corinthians 7:10 NIV).

( )

Properly remembering our past sins with shame will deter us from repeating them and help us receive God's saving grace. When we recall our failures through the lens of Christ's mercy, God produces in us ongoing repentance and deepening humility.

–Robert D. Jones, *Bad Memories*[2]

( )

Our yesterdays present irreparable things to us; it is true that we have lost opportunities which will never return, but God can transform this destructive anxiety into a constructive thoughtfulness for the future. Let the past sleep, but let it sleep on the bosom of Christ. Leave the Irreparable Past in His hands, and step out into the Irresistible Future with Him.

–Oswald Chambers

MY WISDOM KEYS

19

Wisdom and Names

Becoming a Christian is not like becoming a Muslim. You don't have to change your name in order to be in the Church. I want you to understand that the new birth is not a change on your birth certificate; it is a change in your heart. When you are in the presence of God, He will remove the stench of your old character and give you a new one. In this sense we have a name change as it pertains to our character. This is not a work of man, or a typist on a birth certificate. This is a work of the *Holy Spirit*.

(Excerpts from *Insights to Help You Survive Peaks & Valleys*)

Wisdom and Names Reflections

IN the Bible, names were generally significant to the birth, as in *Isaac*, whose name meant "laughter." His mother broke into fits of laughter when she saw what God had done for her in the winter season of her life. On other occasions names were prophetic. The name *Jesus* is prophetic. It means "salvation." Jesus was born to save His people from their sins. In a few cases, the names were relative both to origin and prophecy. A keen example is that of *Moses*, whose name meant "drawn out." He was originally drawn out of the water by Pharaoh's daughter, but prophetically called of God to draw his people out of Egypt.

Understand, then, that a name is important. It tells something about your origin or your destiny. You don't want just anyone to name you. No one should want just anyone to prophesy over him without knowing whether that person is right. Words have power! Many of God's people are walking under the stigma of their old nature's name. That wretched feeling associated with what others called you or thought about you can limit you as you reach for greatness. However, it is not what others think that matters. You want to be sure, even if you are left alone and no one knows but you, to know who the Father says you are. Knowing your new name is for your own edification. When the enemy gets out his list and starts naming your past, tell him, "Haven't you heard? The person you knew died! I am not who he was and I am certainly not what he did!"

Mary, the mother of Jesus, had the baby, but the angel was sent from the Father to give the name. She couldn't name Him because she didn't fully understand His destiny. Don't allow people who don't understand your destiny to name you. They also probably whispered that Jesus was the illegitimate child of Joseph. Maybe there has been some nasty little rumor out on you, too. Rumors smear the reputation and defame the character of many innocent people. However, none lived with any better moral character than Jesus—and they still assaulted His reputation. Just be sure the rumors are false or in the past and keep on living. I often say, "You can't help where you've been, but you can help where you're going."

Points to Ponder

The new birth is not a change on your birth certificate;
it is a change in your heart.

A name is important.

Words have power!

Many of God's people are walking under the stigma
of their old nature's name.

Don't allow people who don't understand your
destiny to name you.

You can't help where you've been,
but you can help where you're going.

Words of Wisdom

To see the world's rebels turned into friends of God is, after all, a God-centered goal. It looks beyond benefit to men. For in coming to Christ their hearts will be changed. They will be made new men throughout. As friends they will do what they would not do as foes. They will lay down their arms and raise their songs of praise: they will *worship* their Creator. They will adore Him whom they once despised. They will praise the Lord!

–Tom Wells, *A Vision for Missions*[1]

...in this rejoice not, that the spirits are subject unto you; but rather rejoice, because your names are written in heaven (Luke 10:20).

The spirit of Jezebel has crept into the Church in America. This Jezebel spirit is leading believers into committing spiritual adultery with her. Unknowingly, the Church is rejecting the fatherhood of God for a marriage to this adulterous spirit.

–Doug Stringer, *Hope for a Fatherless Generation*[2]

Nothing impure will ever enter it, nor will anyone who does what is shameful or deceitful, but only those whose names are written in the Lamb's book of life (Revelation 21:27 NIV).

To be sure, reputations are not always accurate. Yet, in the long run we usually get a reputation that is close to what we deserve. The inner man shows himself often enough that our reputation at least roughly matches our character.

–Dan Doriani, *The Life of a God-Made Man*[3]

MY WISDOM KEYS

20

Wisdom of a Good Attitude

Jealousy is the child of low self-esteem. Then there is always little tiny suicide wrapped in a blanket hiding in the shadows, born in the heart of a person who has been lying in bed with despair or guilt. Then there are people who habitually lie because fantasy seems more exciting than reality. Promiscuity, the child of a twisted need, has an insatiable appetite like that of greed's, which devours all whom it can touch. For all this, you weep through the night. But David said that if we could hold out, joy comes in the morning (see Ps. 30:5).

(Excerpts from *Can You Stand to Be Blessed?*)

Wisdom of a Good Attitude Reflections

THE bad news is, everybody has had a bad night at one time or another. The good news is there will be a morning after. Allow the joy of the morning light to push away any unwanted partners, curses, or fears that stop you from achieving your goal.

So let the hungry mouth of failure's offspring meet the dry breast of a Christian who has determined to overcome the past. In order for these embryos of destruction to survive, they must be fed. They feed on the fears and insecurities of people who haven't declared their liberty. Like a horseleech, they are always sucking the life, the excitement, and the exuberance out of precious moments. The parent is dead; you have laid him to rest, but if not destroyed, the residue of early traumas will attach itself to your successes and abort your missions and goals. It nurses itself in your thought life, feeding off your inner struggles and inhibitions.

Once you realize that you are the source from which it draws its milk, you regain control. Put that baby on a fast! Feed what you want to live and starve what you want to die! Anything you refuse to feed will eventually die. You could literally starve and dehydrate those crying, screaming childhood fears into silence, security, and successful encounters. It's your milk—it's your mind! Why not think positively until every negative thing that is a result of dead issues turns blue and releases its grip on your home and your destiny? It's your mind. You've got the power!

Thoughts are secrets hidden behind quick smiles and professional veneers. They are a private world that others cannot invade. None of us would be comfortable at having all our thoughts played aloud for the whole world to hear. Yet our thoughts can accurately forecast approaching success or failure. No one can hear God think, but we can feel the effects of His thoughts toward us. Like sprouts emerging from enriched soil, our words and eventually our actions push through the fertilized fields of our innermost thoughts. Like our Creator, we deeply affect others by our thoughts toward them.

Points to Ponder

Allow the joy of the morning light to push away any
unwanted partners, curses, or fears that stop
you from achieving your goal.

Think positively until every negative thing that is a result of
dead issues turns blue and releases its grip on your
home and your destiny.

You've got the power!

Your thoughts can accurately forecast
approaching success or failure.

No one can hear God think, but you can feel the
effects of His thoughts toward you.

Words of Wisdom

It's easy to think that once in God's will, everything will fall into place and we'll get from one point to another without any problems. But that's not really how things always work—there are often curves along the way. Miracles come in phases, don't let the enemy shake your confidence.

–Leigh Valentine, *Successfully You!*[1]

Words can never adequately convey the incredible impact of our attitude toward life. The longer I live the more convinced I become that life is 10 percent what happens to us and 90 percent how we respond to it.

–Charles R. Swindoll, *Christian Reader*[2]

For the word of God is living and active. Sharper than any double-edged sword, it penetrates even to dividing soul and spirit, joints and marrow; it judges the thoughts and attitudes of the heart (Hebrews 4:12 NIV).

The attitude within is more important than the circumstances without.

–Author Unknown

Failed government programs and self-sabotaging attitudes will only impede our forward progress. Therefore, we must be constantly willing to rethink and reexamine the vehicles of our past success or lack thereof.

–Reggie White, *Broken Promises, Blinded Dreams*[3]

MY WISDOM KEYS

_____

_____

_____

_____

_____

_____

_____

_____

_____

_____

_____

21

Wisdom to Struggle

I remember so well the early struggles that my wife and I had to maintain our family, finances, and overall well-being while building a ministry. I was working a secular job that God wanted me to leave for full-time ministry. Full-time ministry—what a joke! I was scarcely asked to preach anywhere that offered more than a few pound cakes, a couple jars of jelly, and if I was lucky, enough gas money to get home. My hotel generally would be the back room of some dear elderly church mother who charmingly entertained me as best she could with what she had. It was there, around old coal stoves in tiny churches that never even considered buying a microphone, where I learned how to preach.

(Excerpts from *Insights to Help You to Survive Peaks & Valleys*)

Wisdom to Struggle Reflections

OFTEN I would preach until sweaty and tired, to rows of empty pews with two or three people who decorated the otherwise empty church like earrings placed on the head of a bald doll.

Finally I said yes to full-time ministry. I did it not because I wanted it, but because the company I worked for went out of business and I was forced out of my comfort zone into the land of faith. What a frightening experience it was to find myself without. "Without what?" you ask. I was without everything you could think of: without a job and then a car. Later I was without utilities and often without food. I scraped around doing odd jobs trying to feed two children and a wife without looking like life wasn't working. I thought God had forgotten me. I even preached in suits that shined. They shined not because they were in style, but because they were worn, pressed with an iron, and eventually washed in the washing machine because cleaners were out of the question. I am not ashamed to tell you—in fact I am proud to tell you—that I experienced more about God in those desperate days of struggle as I answered the charges of satan with the perseverance of prayer.

Satan cannot dispute your serving God, but he challenges our reason for serving Him. He says it is for the prominence and protection that God provides. He further insinuates that if things weren't going so well, we would not praise God so fervently. The devil is a liar! We will all face times when we must answer satan's charges and prove that even in the storm, He is still God!

Those early times of challenge sorely tried all that was in me. My pride, my self-esteem, and my self-confidence teetered like a child learning to ride a bicycle.

I learned, however, that if you can remember your beginnings and still reach toward your goals, God will bless you with things without fear of those items becoming idols in your life. Oddly, there is a glory in the agonizing of early years that people who didn't have to struggle seem not to possess. There is a strange sense of competence that comes from being born in the flames of struggle. How wildly exuberant are the first steps of the child who earlier was mobile only through crawling on his hands and knees.

Points to Ponder

Have you found yourself without?

Have you ever thought that God had forgotten about you?

Are you answering the charges of satan
with the perseverance of prayer?

Remember your beginnings and still reach
toward your goals.

God will bless you with things without fear of those items
becoming idols in your life.

There is a strange sense of competence that comes from
being born in the flames of struggle.

Words of Wisdom

Trials come to prove and improve us.

–Augustine

The process of healing and restoration in our marriages takes time. It took years to get to the unhealthy places where we now find ourselves, and even if we think we will unravel them overnight, it usually doesn't happen that way. God will take as much time as is needed to do a thorough job of getting us right.

–Carl Hampsch, *Opposites Attract[1]*

We must combine the toughness of a serpent and the softness of a dove, a tough mind and a tender heart.

–Martin Luther King Jr

Whomever the Lord has adopted and deemed worthy of His fellowship ought to prepare themselves for a hard, toilsome, and unquiet life, crammed with very many and various kinds of evil. It is the Heavenly Father's will thus to exercise them so as to put His own children to a definite test. Beginning with Christ, His first-born, He follows this plan with all His children.

–John Calvin

MY WISDOM KEYS

22

Wisdom and Intent

Many times we wonder why we go through so much persecution. Why do we experience so much rejection that we often feel alienated by those around us just because we love God and want to do His will? God says, "I'm building a solid foundation so you'll better understand pressure and be able to go through the storms of life without being moved or shaken." God's response is simple. Anything that is made well is made slowly. "Quality must go in before the name goes on." Anything that is worth having is worth fighting for and worth working hard for.

(Excerpts from *Power for Living*)

Wisdom and Intent Reflections

WE also have to know that God is not just building any kind of house. God is building a house of glory, a house filled with His Spirit, governed by His Word (will), and submitted to the Lordship of His Son, Jesus Christ. As tenants of that house, we are called to represent the Builder and Lord of that house by manifesting His glory on the earth. God says, "When I get through with you, when I get through nailing on you, when I get through hooking your two-by-fours together and putting windows in, when I get through hanging siding on you and placing bricks on your frame, then you are going to be a glorious edifice, a sight for the world to see." Still the house is not for us to be glorified, but that God might be exalted and glorified. *"But we have this treasure in earthen vessels, that the excellency of the power may be of God, and not of us"* (2 Cor. 4:7).

God's approach to destiny is first establishing the purpose, then reverting to the beginning to develop you and instruct you on how to fulfill the purpose. God works out purpose the way you would design and construct a house. If you wanted to build a massive house, you must first hire an architect. The architect takes the vision you have for the house and transforms it onto paper (blueprint), establishing what it shall be before it is ever built. Then the carpenter comes in and makes the vision a reality by constructing in material form (manifesting in the present) the design (vision) that the architect has established on paper (the blueprint).

Whenever the builder is confused, he refers back to the blueprint. By looking at the blueprint, he knows whether to order steel beams or wood beams, carpet or tile, brick or stucco. Whenever the builder is unclear about any detail or specification, all he needs to do is check the blueprint and look back at what the architect has declared in the design.

I want you to know that God is the Master Architect (designer) and Master Builder all in one. He never gets confused about what is planned or how it is to be built. When God builds something, He builds it for maximum efficiency and optimal performance. We get confused and doubt the outcome. Discouraged, we often find ourselves asking God, "Why did You make me wait while other people go forth? Why does it take so long for my breakthrough to come?" God responds, "What does the blueprint say? What do the specifications call for?"

Points to Ponder

Anything that is worth having is worth fighting for
and worth working hard for.

God is building a house of glory,
a house filled with His Spirit.

God's approach to destiny is first establishing the purpose.

God works out purpose the way you would design and construct a house.

God is the Master Architect (designer)
and Master Builder all in one.

He builds for maximum efficiency and optimal performance.

Words of Wisdom

In His Word He tells you that He sees the unseen. He knows the location of every demon at every moment on earth, 24 hours a day, and He's got your back covered. He's guiding you with His eye to help you avoid peril and pitfalls.

—Steve Shultz, *Can't You Talk Louder God?*[1]

...so is my word that goes out from my mouth: It will not return to me empty, but will accomplish what I desire and achieve the purpose for which I sent it (Isaiah 55:11 NIV).

As we grope our way into the future, we'll learn to come to grips with our marginalization. We'll embrace it and see it as an opportunity for the church to return to her ancient roots in order to reclaim God's original intent for the church.

—Wes Roberts and Glenn C. Marshall, *Reclaiming God's Original Intent for the Church*[2]

When you set an example, you are giving people a pattern to follow. Someone once said, 'Your life speaks so loudly I can't hear what you say.' Your lifestyle is your most powerful message.

—John MacArthur, *The Master's Plan for the Church*[3]

MY WISDOM KEYS

23

Wisdom Through Patience

The problem with most Christians is that we are far too impatient. If God doesn't speak in the first five minutes of our prayer time, we get up, shake ourselves off, and concede that God is not talking today. We no longer have the kind of tenacity, diligence, and persistence like the saints of old. Those saints of bygone days would get on their faces before God and grab hold of the horns of the altar and refuse to let go until they received a sure word from God. Unlike those precious men and women of God, we have become the "microwave" generation. We want everything overnight, even Christian maturity. We want whatever is quick, fast, and in a hurry. We've deleted, erased, and totally obliterated from our Bibles, and our thoughts, those passages of Scripture that command us to wait on God during turbulent, troubling, and unsure times.

(Excerpts from *Power for Living*)

Wisdom Through Patience Reflections

My brethren, count it all joy when ye fall into divers temptations; knowing this, that the trying of your faith worketh patience. But let patience have her perfect work, that ye may be perfect and entire, wanting nothing (James 1:2-4).

YOU might ask me, "Bishop, why (there's that why again) does it often take God so long to answer our prayers?" We put a petition, request, or question before God on a Monday, and it might be the next week or next month before God gives a reply. This tests our faith to see if we will continue to serve God, even if He delays His reply. If God decides to prolong an answer or provision for our needs, are we willing and secure enough in His sovereignty to trust and wait on Him, regardless of how bleak the situation may look? My brothers and sisters, we have to let patience have its perfect (complete, absolute, to full maturity) work.

God's reply to the nagging questions and complex issues that preoccupy our thoughts is, "I may not answer you right away, but go ahead and question why, and wait on Me."

Has God told you that He has destined you for a certain thing? Has God given you a vision of ministry? Has He promised you a particular blessing? Maybe you're single and God has assured you that you'll be married at an appointed time. But it seems as if the mate that God has fitted for your specific needs is nowhere in sight.

"But they that wait upon the Lord shall renew their strength, they shall mount up on wings as eagles; they shall run, and not be weary, and they shall walk, and not faint" (Isa. 40:31). What are you waiting for? I'm waiting for an answer. Does your vision tarry? Wait for it. Be diligent. Don't become weary in well-doing: for in due season you shall reap the reward of your request, your petition, your labor, and the answers to your whys if you faint not (see Gal. 6:9).

Points to Ponder

Christians are far too impatient.

We want everything overnight, even Christian maturity.

If God decides to prolong an answer, are you willing and
secure enough to trust and wait on Him?

Allow patience to have its perfect
(complete, absolute, to full maturity) work.

Don't become weary in well doing.

In due season you will reap the reward of your request, your
petition, your labor, and the answers to your questions.

Words of Wisdom

Let us not become weary in doing good, for at the proper time we will reap a harvest if we do not give up (Galatians 6:9 NIV).

We spend a lot of time in our lives waiting because change is a process. Many people want change, but they don't want to go through the waiting process. But the truth is, waiting is a given—we are going to wait. The question is, are we going to wait the wrong or right way? If we wait the wrong way, we'll be miserable; but if we decide to wait God's way, we can become patient and enjoy the wait. It takes practice, but as we let God help us in each situation, we develop patience, which is one of the most important Christian virtues.

–Joyce Meyer[1]

And not only so, but we glory in tribulations also: knowing that tribulation worketh patience; and patience, experience; and experience, hope: and hope maketh not ashamed; because the love of God is shed abroad in our hearts by the Holy Ghost which is given unto us (Romans 5:3-5).

The faith of Christ offers no buttons to push for quick service. The new order must wait the Lord's own time, and that is too much for the man in a hurry. He just gives up and becomes interested in something else.

–A.W. Tozer

MY WISDOM KEYS

_____

_____

_____

_____

_____

_____

_____

_____

_____

_____

_____

_____

_____

24

Wisdom and Compassion

I am concerned that we maintain our compassion. How can we be in the presence of a loving God and then not love little ones? When Jesus blessed the children, He challenged the adults to become as children. Oh, to be a child again, to allow ourselves the kind of relationship with God that we may have missed as a child. Sometimes we need to allow the Lord to adjust the damaged places of our past. I am glad to say that God provides arms that allow grown children to climb up like children and be nurtured through the tragedies of early days. Isn't it nice to toddle into the presence of God and let Him hold you in His arms?

(Excerpts from *Power for Living*)

Wisdom and Compassion Reflections

IN God, we can become children again. Salvation is God giving us a chance to start over again. He will not abuse the children who come to Him. Through praise, I approach Him like a toddler on unskillful legs. In worship, I kiss His face and am held by the caress of His anointing. He has no ulterior motive, for His caress is safe and wholesome. It is so important that we learn how to worship and adore Him, for in both is power for living. There is no better way to climb into His arms. Even if you were exposed to grown-up situations when you were a child, God can reverse what you've been through. He'll let the grown-up person experience the joy of being a child in the presence of God!

Reach out and embrace the fact that God has been watching over you all of your life. He covers you, He clothes you, and He blesses you! Rejoice in Him in spite of the broken places. God's grace is sufficient for your needs and your scars. He will anoint you with oil. The anointing of the Lord be upon you now! May it bathe, heal, and strengthen you as never before.

If great things came from those who never suffered, we might think that they accomplished those things of their own accord. When a broken person submits to God, God gets the glory for the wonderful things He accomplishes—no matter how far that person has fallen. The anointing of God restores us and allows us to accomplish great and noble things. Believe it!

The hidden Christ that's been locked up behind your fears, your problems, and your insecurity, will come forth in your life. You will see the power of the Lord Jesus do a mighty thing.

Points to Ponder

Allow the Lord to adjust the damaged places of your past.

Toddle into the presence of God and let Him
hold you in His arms.

His caress is safe and wholesome.

Embrace the fact that God has been watching
over you all of your life.

The anointing of God restores you and allows you to
accomplish great and noble things.

Believe it!

Words of Wisdom

Love your fellowmen, and cry about them if you cannot bring them to Christ. If you cannot save them, you can weep over them. If you cannot give them a drop of cold water in hell, you can give them your heart's tears while they are still in this body.

–C.H. Spurgeon

But thou, O Lord, art a God full of compassion, and gracious, long suffering, and plenteous in mercy and truth (Psalm 86:15).

Jesus' boat landed near a large expanse of grass. He went to the top of a small hill to pray. But soon the multitudes gathered at the hill. When Jesus saw the people, as always, His heart was moved.

–Elmer L. Towns, *Praying the Gospels.*[1]

Compassion is the deep feeling of sharing in the suffering of another and the desire to relieve that suffering.

–Jerry Bridges, *Trusting God*[2]

MY WISDOM KEYS

_____

_____

_____

_____

_____

_____

_____

_____

_____

_____

_____

_____

25

Wisdom Sirens

Normally, anytime there is a crash, there is an injury. If one person collides with another, they generally damage everything associated with them. In the same way, a crashing relationship affects everyone associated with it, whether it is in a corporate office, a ministry, or a family. That jarring and shaking does varying degrees of damage to everyone involved. Whether we like to admit it or not, we are affected by the actions of others to various degrees. The amount of the effect, though, depends on the nature of the relationship.

(Excerpts from *Power for Living*)

Wisdom Sirens Reflections

WHAT is important is the fact that we don't have to die in the crashes and collisions of life. We must learn to live life with a seat belt in place, even though it is annoying to wear. Similarly, we need spiritual and emotional seat belts as well. We don't need the kind that harness us in and make us live like a mannequin; rather, we need the kind that are invisible, but greatly appreciated in a crash.

Inner assurance is the seat belt that stops you from going through the roof when you are rejected. It is inner assurance that holds you in place. It is the assurance that God is in control and that what He has determined no one can disallow! If He said He was going to bless you, then disregard the mess and believe a God who cannot lie. The rubbish can be cleared and the bruises can be healed. Just be sure that when the smoke clears, you are still standing. You are too important to the purpose of God to be destroyed by a situation that is only meant to give you character and direction. No matter how painful, devastated, or disappointed you may feel, you are still here. Praise God, for He will use the cornerstone developed through rejections and failed relationships to perfect what He has prepared!

Lift your voice above the screaming sirens and alarms of men whose hearts have panicked! Lift your eyes above the billowing smoke and spiraling emotions. Pull yourself up—it could have killed you, but it didn't. Announce to yourself, "I am alive. I can laugh. I can cry, and by God's grace, I can survive!"

When Jesus encountered the infirm woman of Luke chapter 13, He called out to her. There may have been many fine women present that day, but the Lord didn't call them forward. He reached around all of them and found that crippled woman in the back. He called forth the wounded, hurting woman with a past. He issued the Spirit's call to those who had their value and self-esteem destroyed by the intrusion of vicious circumstances.

Points to Ponder

A crashing relationship affects everyone associated with it.

Inner assurance is the seat belt that stops you from going through the roof when you are rejected.

You are too important to the purpose of God to be destroyed by a situation that is only meant to give you character and direction.

God, will use the cornerstone developed through rejections and failed relationships to perfect what He has prepared!

Announce to yourself, "I am alive. I can laugh. I can cry, and by God's grace, I can survive!"

Words of Wisdom

Ultimately, prosperity is a state of mind. It is a mindset developed by constant focus on what is good and right for your life.

–Noel Jones and Scott Chaplan, *Vow of Prosperity*[1]

Love does not delight in evil but rejoices with the truth. It always protects, always trusts, always hopes, always perseveres (1 Corinthians 13:6-7 NIV).

It is the Holy Spirit who is causing you to persevere. In those times when you are lazy and have no enthusiasm for any Spiritual Discipline, or when you haven't practiced a particular Discipline as you habitually do, it is the Holy Spirit who prompts you to pick it up in spite of your feelings. Left to yourself, you would have forsaken these means of sustaining grace long ago, but the Holy Spirit preserves you by granting to you the grace to persevere in them.

–Donald Whitney, *Spiritual Disciplines for the Christian Life*[2]

There are many causes of rejection: abuse (including physical, verbal, sexual, emotional), turmoil within the home, adoption, abandonment, unfaithfulness in marriage, divorce, peer rejection, etc. And there are many results.

–Joyce Meyer, *The Root of Rejection*[3]

MY WISDOM KEYS

26

Wisdom and Anointed People

Anointed people are in great demand by those who need the touch of God in their lives. Because anointed people have the ability to draw from the resources of God's miracle-working power in time of desperate need, people have a tendency to worship and make idols out of them. But God says He shares His glory with no one. God is a jealous God (see Exod. 20:5). God will not bestow His Holy Spirit upon some flaky, selfish Christian who is engrossed with selfish ambition, trying to build a kingdom at the expense of using God's anointing. Many ministries try to build their own personal kingdom, while rationalizing that they are building God's Church. The devil is a liar and the truth is not in him (see John 8:44).

(Excerpts from *Power for Living*)

Wisdom and Anointed People Reflections

WHY are the anointed persecuted? Anointed people are free people. The Word of God says where the Spirit of the Lord is there is liberty (see 2 Cor. 3:17). Wicked leadership and stubborn, sedate people, who have taken counsel against the Lord, do not like free people, because free people can't be controlled.

Anointed people are full of the Holy Ghost. Life in the Holy Ghost is righteousness, peace, and joy. Anointed people are people who have been burdened by the cross of Calvary and are no longer bound by the sins and embarrassments of old lifestyles.

Anointed men and women of God know that because of the precious blood shed by Jesus Christ; they have right-standing with the Father—they possess power for living. When they think about the goodness of Jesus, and all that He's done for them, their very soul cries out, "Hallelujah!" They begin to praise God with unrestrained zeal and passion. That, my brothers and sisters, is what gives you joy unspeakable and full of glory, the anointed presence of the Holy Spirit.

Controlling people (like those rulers who wanted to keep the people from praising Jesus) find that type of ecstatic praise to be very irritating and irrational. They want you to be composed and dignified at all times. Why? Because instead of giving praise and worship to Jesus, they unknowingly (and some knowingly) want you to praise them—the great "Doctor So-and-So" and the wonderful "Mother Who-dun-it." But again, the devil is a liar!

The anointing of God has the innate and wonderful ability to soften hard hearts, break stiff necks, crush pride, and tear down the walls of strife and division. This inevitably will bring sincere men and women to repentance. A repented heart is soft and gentle. Gentle hearts are receptive to reconciliation. Reconciliation is the hallmark of love. Love and forgiveness are the cornerstone and foundation that build.

Points to Ponder

Anointed people have the ability to draw from the resources of God's miracle-working power.

God will not bestow His Holy Spirit upon some flaky, selfish Christian who is engrossed with selfish ambition.

Anointed people are free people.

Anointed people are full of the Holy Ghost.

The anointing of God has the innate and wonderful ability to soften hard hearts.

A repented heart is soft and gentle.

Words of Wisdom

There are several scriptural references which mention the prophets as being madmen or fools. However, a closer study shows that these designations are the contentions of the prophets' critics who assert this of them in mockery.

–James W. Goll, *Shifting Shadows of Supernatural Experiences*[1]

Now it is God who makes both us and you stand firm in Christ. He anointed us, set his seal of ownership on us, and put his Spirit in our hearts as a deposit, guaranteeing what is to come (2 Corinthians 1:21-22 NIV).

Are we under His authority, or our own? You can't "yes, but" to Scripture. He said it, or He didn't say it. And we either obey, or we do not. It is not we who have the authority. It is the Lord. His name is Jesus and His title is "the Christ." And He has it all. He will share it with no one.

–Cal Thomas, "The Authority of the State," *Tabletalk*[2]

A soul in this state seeks nothing for itself, but all for God. Some may say, 'What, then, does this soul?' It leaves itself to be conducted by God's providences and creatures. Outwardly, its life seems quite common; inwardly, it is wholly resigned to the divine will.

–Madame Jeanne-Marie Bouvier de la Motte-Guyon, *Autobiography of Madame Guyon*[3]

MY WISDOM KEYS

27

Wisdom and the Presence of God

There is no tiptoeing around the presence of God with pristine daintiness—as if we could tiptoe softly enough not to awaken a God who never sleeps nor slumbers. We shuffle in His presence like children who were instructed not to disturb their father, although God isn't sleepy and He doesn't have to go to work. He is alive and awake, and He is well. We blare like trumpets announcing our successes, but we whisper our failures through parched lips in the shadows of our relationship with Him. We dare not air our inconsistencies with arrogance because we know we are so underdeveloped and dependent upon Him for everything we need.

(Excerpts from *Power for Living*)

Wisdom and the Presence of God Reflections

T is the nature of a fallen humanity to hide from God. Adam hid from God. How ridiculous it is for us to think that we can hide from Him! His intelligence supersedes our frail ability to be deceptive. Adam hid himself. No wonder we are lost. We have hidden ourselves. We didn't hide our work or our gifts; we have hidden ourselves.

When a person hides himself from God, he loses himself. What good is it to know where everything else is, if we cannot find ourselves? Our loss causes a desperation that produces sin and separation. Like the prodigal son in chapter 15 of Luke, in our desperation we need to come to ourselves and come out from under the bushes where we have hidden ourselves. We need to become transparent in the presence of the Lord.

Adam's meager attempt at morality caused him to sew together a few leaves in a figgy little apron that was dying even while he was sewing it. Why would a lost man cover himself with leaves? Adam said, "I was afraid." Fear separated this son from his Father; fear caused him to conspire to deceive his only Solution. This fear was not reverence—it was desperation.

If Adam had only run *toward* instead of *away* from God, he could have been delivered! Why, then, do we continue to present a God who cannot be approached to a dying world? Many in the Christian family are still uncomfortable with their heavenly

Father. Some Christians do not feel accepted in the Beloved. They feel that their relationship with God is meritorious, but they are intimidated because of His holiness. I admit that His holiness all the more exposes our flawed, soiled personhood. Yet His grace allows us to approach Him—though we are not worthy—through the bloody skins soaked with Christ's blood.

Points to Ponder

When you hide yourself from God, you lose yourself.

You need to become transparent in the presence of the Lord.

Fear separates you from your Father God.

Run *toward* instead of *away* from God, and be delivered!

Don't be intimidated because of His holiness.

His grace allows us to approach Him
through the blood of Christ.

Words of Wisdom

But there is a more specific type of His Presence—His Manifest Presence. God's Manifest Presence is revealed whenever He makes Himself real to *you*, personally. This takes place when He makes Himself real to you *in your spirit* and you know beyond a shadow of a doubt that God has spoken to your heart. You know He has manifested Himself to you; you are experiencing His Manifest Presence.

–Don Nori Sr., *Manifest Presence*[1]

To step into the realm of faith takes one beyond the "veil" of the curtain and beyond the "veil" of the humanity of Jesus. It gives us eyes by which we can see transcendence in the face of the natural, and the extraordinary in the face of the ordinary.

–Dr. Francis J. Sizer, *Into His Presence*[2]

And they heard the voice of the Lord God walking in the garden in the cool of the day: and Adam and his wife hid themselves from the presence of the Lord God amongst the trees of the garden (Genesis 3:8).

Moses, David, and Paul—three voices raised in holy des-peration, in pursuit of the presence of the living God. All three were men of action, men of activity, men who led nations and changed history. Yet at the core of their being, there was a cry for His holy presence.

–Robert Stearns, *Prepare the Way (or Get Out of the Way!)*[3]

MY WISDOM KEYS

28

Wisdom in the Wilderness

When you speak of the wilderness, your mind immediately imagines a dry place where nothing green grows. Everything in the wilderness is brown and unappealing to the eye. The environment of the wilderness is not brightened with any color. Everything in the wilderness has adapted itself to live in this type of climate. Rarely does it rain in the wilderness, and when it does, plants store the moisture they need because there is no guarantee when it will rain again. When we are going through our wilderness experience, we must be like the trees and the other animals of the wilderness. We must learn to adapt our faith to the challenges a wilderness brings.

(Excerpts from *Water in the Wilderness*)

Wisdom in the Wilderness Reflections

THE animals in the wilderness have learned to travel and hunt at night because it is cooler at night. Spiritually, we too must learn to find a place where the Lord can minister to us in our wilderness. It is a place where He can give us instruction about what to do next. Like the trees that store up water, uncertain of when it will rain again, we must store up His Word in our hearts. Many of us are living in the wilderness for various reasons.

The wilderness is a place of dying, where all the things that cause you to stumble in your walk with God are killed. If you have ever watched a movie where people dared to enter the wilderness with little or no understanding of life in the wilderness, they often did not survive there. Since they had no one to help or advise them, they tried to fight the elements in their own strength.

Likewise, many of us have been in the wilderness and we have tried unsuccessfully to fight the battle in our own strength. You see, the wilderness is a place where God says, "I finally have you in a place where I can speak to you."

Do not be fooled into thinking that you can ever be fully prepared for life in the wilderness. Sometimes, God leads us abruptly into the wilderness. He might have been trying to get you to come to Him or to get you to take your spiritual life more seriously. Perhaps He has been trying to draw your attention to the call He has placed in your life.

God loves you so much that He is willing to take just that type of risk on you. He knows that you may either serve Him or reject Him. You may say, "Lord, wherever You lead, I will follow, even through the wilderness." Or you may decide to say, "I can't deal with this. I thought life would be better than this. I quit."

But God knows that we must be tried in the fire so that we can become as pure as gold. God brings us into the wilderness to perfect our faith.

Points to Ponder

When you are going through a wilderness experience, learn to adapt your faith to the challenges a wilderness brings.

Find a place where the Lord can minister to you in the wilderness.

The wilderness is a place of dying, where all the things that cause you to stumble in your walk with God are killed.

He might have been trying to get you to come to Him or to get you to take your spiritual life more seriously.

God brings you into the wilderness to perfect your faith.

Words of Wisdom

Thus they went on till they came to the place where the strait way touches the foot of a skull-shaped hill. This was this hill they had been beholding all along their journey. But oh, how much more it touched their hearts to come to the very place of sacrifice. 'Twas here that Christian's burden had tumbled from off His back and now, 'twas here that other burdens tumbled and more tears made their way down other faces.

–John Bunyan, *Pilgrim's Progress, Part 2 Christiana*[1]

He said, 'I am the voice of one crying in the wilderness, Make straight the way of the Lord, as said the prophet Esaias' (John 1:23).

Today the Muslim people continue in this wilderness at the point of death. Once again, in this spiritual wilderness, there is a well that they cannot see. They have no father to give them bread or water. At the same time, the Church is walking away from them, unable to watch them die.

–Faisal Malick, *The Destiny of Islam in the Endtimes*[2]

Though my natural instinct is to wish for a life free from pain, trouble, and adversity, I am learning to welcome anything that makes me conscious of my need for Him. If prayer is birthed out of desperation, then anything that makes me desperate for God is a blessing.

–Nancy Leigh DeMoss, *A Place of Quiet Rest*[3]

MY WISDOM KEYS

29

Wisdom Over the Enemy

The enemy fights those who know who they are and whose they are. The Bible affirms that God is faithful (see 1 Cor. 1:9). The Word of God states, *"But to us there is but one God, the Father, of whom are all things, and we in him; and one Lord Jesus Christ, by whom are all things, and we by him"* (1 Cor. 8:6).

(Excerpts from *Water in the Wilderness*)

Wisdom Over the Enemy Reflections

ARE you aware that the more the enemy fights you, the greater the indication that blessings are on the way? You must be cognizant of this fact as a Christian. If you do not know that about life, you cannot make it. You have got to know that it is because you are on the verge of a miracle that the devil is fighting you. He is fighting you so hard because you are getting closer to your deliverance, and the closer you get, the greater the struggle.

If you hold out a little while longer, God's going to give you the victory in every circumstance of your life. I am learning to be encouraged when I meet with obstacles because I see them as an indication of a fresh move of God in my life.

When people ask you who your God is, how do you respond? With confidence, your shoulders held high, and a smile on your face you can say, "He is everything I will ever need. He is my Father, the Creator of Heaven and Earth, and the One who sustains the universe. He is Jehovah, the I am that I am."

When you are in the wilderness, you must find out what the plan of God is for you. You cannot rely on anyone else's plan. Only a plan from God will suffice in the wilderness.

God has not promised that you will not go through hardship, neither has He promised that you will not experience adversity. But listen to what He says: "When you pass through the waters, I will be with you. When you go through the flood, I'll be there. Should you have to go through fire, I will be there. As I was with Shadrach, Meshach, and Abednego, so will I be with you. I will be the fourth One in the furnace."

I am very grateful that the Lord's been walking with me all these years. I say this not because I have not been through anything, or that I have not faced various challenges and dark moments in life, but I do recognize that the Lord has been the fourth One in the fiery furnace. He has protected me from the scorching of the flames. When the pressure and the flames seemed as if they would engulf me, His words of assurance would comfort me.

Points to Ponder

The enemy fights those who know who they are
and whose they are.

The more the enemy fights you, the greater the indication
that blessings are on the way.

God's going to give you the victory in every
circumstance of your life.

Only a plan from God will suffice in the wilderness.

Recognize that the Lord has been the fourth
One in the fiery furnace.

Allow His words of assurance to comfort you.

Words of Wisdom

If you are going to successfully affect the power of the enemy, his authority, his seat, and his throne, you are going to have to know his weapons.

–Dr. Lynn Hiles, *The Revelation of Jesus Christ*[1]

The enemy will not see you vanish into God's company without an effort to reclaim you.

–C.S. Lewis

These things I have spoken unto you, that in me ye might have peace. In the world ye shall have tribulation: but be of good cheer; I have overcome the world" (John 16:33).

...war seems to be a primary weapon that the devil uses to steal, kill, and destroy the creature man, created in God's image. It is clear that an orphan spirit, or spirit of alienation, has been powerfully sown into the human psyche as a result of war.

–Fred and Sharon Wright, *The World's Greatest Revivals*[2]

MY WISDOM KEYS

30

Wisdom and Praise

Praise is magnifying and exalting the Lord in our hearts. Praise is glorifying the Lord with the fruit of our lips. When we begin to praise God with all our heart, we lose sight of the magnitude of our problems as we gain a vision of the greatness of our Lord.

(Excerpts from *Water in the Wilderness*)

Wisdom and Praise Reflections

I N order to truly praise God, we must learn to go beyond ourselves and our human limitations. Many times when the enemies of Israel encamped around them, God told Joshua to send out the tribe of Judah first. Judah means praise. Judah marched before the enemies of Israel, armed with nothing but instruments of praise.

When the tribe of Judah began to praise God with their whole heart, God set ambushes among the enemy and confused them. The same principle happens in the spirit realm. When we really begin to praise God, our praise confounds the enemy, and demonic forces begin to withdraw their power and influence.

> *For though we walk in the flesh we do not war after the flesh: (For the weapons of our warfare are not carnal, but mighty through God to the pulling down of strongholds;) Casting down imaginations, and every high thing that exalteth itself against the knowledge of God, and bringing into captivity every thought to the obedience of Christ* (2 Corinthians 10:3-5).

Praise and worship is the most profound way of expressing our love to the Father. God loves to be praised and worshiped. However, in order to praise God, we must understand the power that praise and worship wield. Praise and worship can break demonic strongholds that have bound us.

Praise and the Word of God are able to pull down strongholds. There is power in praise and worship. Let us pause here to examine this concept of praise as a weapon against spiritual strongholds.

The erection of strongholds takes place in our thought process. For example, suppose you were visiting a new church where their method of praise and worship is somewhat different from yours. Immediately, your mind tells you that their way is wrong, or, worse still, that they are not saved. This is a stronghold. Remember that a stronghold is a belief system that is contrary to what God's Word says. You see, in this case, your church has spoken against being too expressive in worship and praise. To them praise and worship does not have to be loud and noisy.

Points to Ponder

When you praise God with all your heart, you lose sight of the magnitude of your problems.

When you praise God, you will gain a vision of the greatness of your Lord.

To truly praise God, learn to go beyond yourself and your human limitations.

A stronghold is a belief system that is contrary to what God's Word says.

Praise and the Word of God pull down spiritual strongholds.

There is power in praise and worship.

Words of Wisdom

Make a joyful noise unto the Lord, all the earth: make a loud noise, and rejoice, and sing praise. (Psalm 98:4)

This is when praise becomes more than a chore or duty. You don't have to work up your praise because it automatically bubbles up from with you.

–Myles Munroe, *The Purpose and Power of Praise and Worship*[1]

The same holds true today. To offer to God our talents and service is to praise Him in the marketplace, at school, at home, and everywhere else on earth—as long as we do it unto the Lord, as we are admonished in Scripture (see Colossians 3:23).

–Mark A. Brewer, *What's Your Spiritual Quotient?*[2]

Witnessing a magnificent fireworks display, hearing a stunning symphony, or seeing a glorious sunset can evoke a response of praise. But often, it's easier to praise a sunset than the Creator of the sunset. In that same way, the difficulties of life often cloud our vision and keep us from praising God. What can we do to restore a heart-attitude of praise?

–*Keys to Powerful Living: Praise*[3]

MY WISDOM KEYS

31

Wisdom and Music

God loves music. He said, "If you want Me to move, play Me some music. Get Me somebody who has an instrument." When Saul was possessed with demons, David played his harp until the demons left Saul. There is something about the anointed music of the Holy Spirit.

(Excerpts from *Water in the Wilderness*)

Wisdom and Music Reflections

ANOINTED music will drive out demons, trouble, and sickness. That is why you must be very careful about the type of music that you allow to enter your soul for it has a great effect on your inner man (spirit man). Get some anointed and powerful music. If you want your body to be healed, get some music that speaks healing into your body. Elisha said, "Get me somebody who will play me a song." The Bible says that when the minstrel began to play, the Word of the Lord began to flow out of Elisha's mouth.

Don't you allow anyone to take your song from your lips. You may lose friends, but don't lose your song. You might not sing well in the hearing of other people, but keep your song. You might croak like a frog, but keep your song. David said, "Make a joyful noise unto God, all ye lands" (Psalm 66:1). Paul demonstrated that if you have a song, you can sing your way out of the jail. If you have a song, you can encourage yourself. Even when there is nobody around to encourage you, and you feel all alone, if you have a song you can encourage yourself in the Lord.

God will move when you start praising Him. When you start to praise God, He will come in the middle of your drought, in the middle of your wilderness, and in the middle of your dry place, and say, "I've got a plan!"

Thou shalt worship the Lord thy God, and him only shalt thou serve (Matthew 4:10).

Whatever we worship is what we ultimately will end up serving. Our nature demands that we worship something. What we worship is up to us.

> *But the hour cometh, and now is, when the true worshippers shall worship the Father in spirit and in truth: for the Father seeketh such to worship him* (John 4:23).

Points to Ponder

God loves music.

Anointed music will drive out demons,
trouble, and sickness.

Don't you allow anyone to take your song from your lips.

If you have a song you can encourage yourself in the Lord.

When you praise God, He will come to you.

What you worship is up to you.

Words of Wisdom

Then David and all the house of Israel played music before the Lord on all kinds of instruments of fir wood, on harps, on stringed instruments, on tambourines, on sistrums, and on cymbals (2 Samuel 6:5 NKJV).

Lord I lift Your name on high.
Lord I love to sing Your praises.
I'm so glad You're in my life.
I'm so glad You came to save us.

–SonicFlood[1]

He was leaping and dancing and shouting praises to God. The worships saw him walking and leaping and recognized he was the lame man who begged at the gate. So the crowd was surprised and curious.

–Elmer Towns, *Praying the Book of Acts*[2]

So I'm taking a stand—and I hope others will—to really live what I believe and embrace who I am in Jesus Christ. And then I believe we are called to just get with it. We are called to share our joy by serving the lost. The poor. The sick. The brokenhearted. The least of these. In Christ, we are given the courage and strength to change the world.

–Michael W. Smith, top-selling Christian recording artist[3]

MY WISDOM KEYS

32

Wisdom and Worship

To experience true worship you must first develop a relationship with the Father. All relationships are dependent upon good communication. For us as believers, prayer is the means of communicating with the Father. This relationship can be likened to that of a man and his wife. There is the sense of intimacy, closeness, and oneness. It is the closeness that you should never share with anyone else.

(Excerpts from *Water in the Wilderness*)

Wisdom and Worship Reflections

WHEN a man and a woman first get married, their relationship is new and exists on that level of looking deeply into each other's eyes. This is the honeymoon stage. At this stage, each worships the ground that the other walks on. Their focus is on each other. But, as time goes on, the honey dries a little and the moon begins to lose its luster. The newness in their relationship begins to wear off, giving way to a different dimension in their relationship.

They begin to know each other on a more intimate level. They can feel each other's hurts and desires. They avoid what will hurt or jeopardize their closeness. They don't hide anything; rather, they express their feelings in confidence and trust. They trust each other with their weaknesses and shortcomings, confident that they will not be used against them. This is the kind of desire that the Lord wants us to enjoy with Him, a close relationship that leads to intimate worship.

There are different kinds of gods we may find ourselves bowing to. Some of us worship our children. Some worship money. Some worship sin. Some worship themselves while others worship all types of things: a paycheck or reputation, for example.

Have you ever observed a Christian who recently got saved? He worships God with a deep gratitude for his salvation. The first stage in the romance of a man and woman is often referred to as infatuation. This is also typical of the first stage of our relationship with Christ. The dictionary describes *infatuation* as "to behave foolishly, to inspire with foolish and unreasoning love or attachment." However, as we mature in the Lord, this type of attraction takes on a new and higher dimension. Infatuation, like romance, operates more on feelings than reality, on the external than on the internal. It is more fleeting than stable, more inconsistent than constant.

But mature love is consistent because it is based on commitment. Commitment (covenant) is what sustains any lasting and stable relationship.

Points to Ponder

To experience true worship you must first develop a
relationship with the Father.

The Lord wants you to enjoy with Him a close
relationship that leads to intimate worship.

Worship God with a deep gratitude for your salvation.

As you mature in the Lord, your attraction takes on
a new and higher dimension.

Mature love is consistent because it is
based on commitment.

Commitment will sustain a stable relationship.

Words of Wisdom

Worship cannot be isolated or relegated to just one place, time, or segment of our lives. We cannot verbally thank and praise God while living lives of selfishness and carnality. That kind of effort at worship is a perversion. Real acts of worship must be the overflow of a worshiping life... As God warms the heart with righteousness and love, the resulting life of praise that boils over is the truest expression of worship.

–John MacArthur, *The Ultimate Priority*[1]

We must, during all our labor and in all else we do, even in our reading and writing, holy though both may be—I say more, even during our formal devotions and spoken prayers—pause for some short moment, as often indeed as we can, to worship God in the depth of our heart, to savor Him, though it be but in passing, and as it were by stealth. Since you are not unaware that God is present before you whatever you are doing, that He is at the depth and centre of your soul, why not then pause from time to time at least from that which occupies you outwardly, even from your spoken prayers, to worship Him inwardly, to praise Him, petition Him, to offer Him your heart and thank Him? What can God have that gives Him greater satisfaction than that a thousand times a day all His creatures should thus pause to withdraw and worship Him in the heart?

–Brother Lawrence

I can safely say, on the authority of all that is revealed in the Word of God, that any man or woman on this earth who is bored and turned off by worship is not ready for heaven.

–A.W. Tozer.

God is Spirit, and those who worship Him must worship in spirit and truth (John 4:24 NKJV).

MY WISDOM KEYS

33

Wisdom of Second Chances

The heavenly Father is always willing to give His unrepentant children the opportunity to turn to Him completely, without reservation or restriction. All we have to do is confess our sins before Him, assured that He is *'faithful and just to forgive us our sins, and to cleanse us from all unrighteousness'* (1 John 1:9). God's desire is not to condemn, but to redeem.

(Excerpts from *The Harvest*)

Wisdom of Second Chances Reflections

There is therefore now no condemnation to them which are in Christ Jesus, who walk not after the flesh, but after the Spirit. For the law of the Spirit of life in Christ Jesus hath made me free from the law of sin and death (Romans 8:1-2).

GOD is always willing to forgive and restore, as long as He knows that we are sincere and that our hearts are open toward Him.

King David, an adulterer and a murderer, repented of his sin and found God's loving kindness and His mercies new every morning.

God's love toward His children is so great that He continues to stretch forth His hand, extending it the second, third, and fourth time, until we get our hearts right with Him.

All I needed was a chance. When I heard the Word of God speaking to my heart to come out of the world, I climbed out of sin in a hurry. When I told my friends good-bye, they laughed at me. In fact, they continue to mock my ministry, imitating the way I praise and worship God.

That doesn't bother me, because the same Holy Spirit I received years ago, is still real and present in my life today. He keeps me alive, holy, and righteous before God without blame!

While my friends are shooting up, snorting drugs, getting arrested, going to jail, and living in sin, I'm free, shouting and praising God. I'm enjoying the liberty, joy, and peace of abundant life in the Lord Jesus Christ. I'm happily married, raising godly children, prospering, and going forth proclaiming the Gospel.

When God blesses you, not only will He bless you personally, but He will bless your family, your field, your crops, and your land. According to Deuteronomy 28, God will take you—who used to be the tail—and make you the head.

When all of your former friends are miserable and dying with needles in their arms, you can have joy in your heart, peace in your mind, and victory over the lust of the flesh. God, and God alone, can and will do that for you. He is the God of the second chance.

Points to Ponder

God's desire is not to condemn, but to redeem.

God is always willing to forgive and restore.

God's love toward His children is great.

God keeps you alive, holy, and righteous without blame.

God will bless you personally in many ways.

He is the God of the second chance.

Words of Wisdom

He [Jesus] told her everything about her that might cause a holy person to stay away from her (such as the fact that she was a multiple divorcee and was currently living in conjugal relations outside of wedlock), and He offered her abundant life just for acknowledging Him as the Source of all holiness.

–James Wilson, *Living as Ambassadors of Relationships*[1]

And the Lord turned, and looked upon Peter, and Peter remembered the word of the Lord, how He had said unto him, before the cock crows, thou shalt deny Me thrice (Luke 22:61).

And I say also unto thee, that thou art Peter, and upon this rock I will build My church; and the gates of hell shall not prevail against it (Matthew 16:18).

Our Lord and Master Jesus Christ, in saying, Repent Ye, intended that the whole of the life of believers should be repentance.

–Martin Luther, *First of 95 Theses*

MY WISDOM KEYS

34

Wisdom of Now

Seeing the wonders of God should cause us to consider the awesomeness of God and how we, as humans, fit into His divine scheme of things. Observing the balance of the universe should lead us to conclude there is no one like God, and His very existence demands that we worship Him while we live on His earth.

(Excerpts from *The Harvest*)

Wisdom of Now Reflections

HUMANISM is no more than man's feeble attempt to put himself on God's level. Only a sinful man, however, would be foolish enough to do so.

The apostle Paul describes people who claim to be religious but refuse to worship God:

When they knew God, they glorified Him not as God, neither were thankful; but became vain in their imaginations, and their foolish heart was darkened. Professing themselves to be wise, they became fools (Romans 1:21-22).

Wouldn't it be terrible to discover there had been a time of great and wonderful harvest, and you, through ignorance and disobedience, were not part of it? Nothing creates more regret than knowing something wonderful happened and realizing that you missed it. "I was about to turn my life around; I was thinking about giving my life to God, but I just acted too late."

Maybe you even expressed to friends and relatives, "You know, I have been thinking about getting saved!"

But when they laughed and said, "You're just playing the religious game," you decided at the last minute not to commit your life to Jesus.

Now you find yourself lost and without God.

"I was thinking about it," you say, "but there are some things I want to do first, some pleasures I haven't yet experienced."

With deep regret, you wonder, "I don't know why I didn't come to the Lord. I had an opportunity to give my heart to Jesus, and I just sat there on the verge of yielding. I felt like it. I even grabbed the front of the pew; I started to stand up. I don't know why I didn't. I don't know what kept me in my seat, but I thought it was too soon. Maybe next week."

You waited, and now the harvest has passed.

Jeremiah, declared, *"The harvest is passed, the summer is ended, and* [still] *we are not saved"* (Jer. 8:20).

Sinner-man or woman, boy or girl, don't miss this harvest. Don't let it pass you by! You may never get another chance. Another harvest may not knock at your door again. Arise now and give your life to Jesus Christ.

Points to Ponder

There is no one like God.

His very existence demands that you worship Him.

Have you made a commitment to God?

Are you part of His great harvest?

Don't let it pass you by!

Arise now and give your life to Jesus Christ.

Words of Wisdom

When God is in my space and your space, when we allow God into the closed areas of our lives, we can find our true selves.

–Derek Knoke, *God in MySpace*[1]

( )

For whosoever shall call upon the name of the Lord shall be saved (Romans 10:13).

( )

On January 12, 1723, I made a solemn dedication of myself to God, and wrote it down; giving up myself, and all that I had to God; to be for the future, in no respect, my own; to act as one that had no right to be himself, in any respect. And solemnly vowed to take God for my whole portion and felicity; looking on nothing else, as any part of my happiness, nor acting as if it were; and His law for the constant rule of my obedience: engaging to fight against the world, the flesh, and the devil, to the end of my life.

–Jonathan Edwards

( )

When people are right with God, they are apt to be hard on themselves and easy on other people. But when they are not right with God, they are easy on themselves and hard on others.

–John Newton

MY WISDOM KEYS

_____

_____

_____

_____

_____

_____

_____

_____

_____

_____

_____

_____

_____

35

Wisdom Versus False Teachings

The Bible says in the end times, or latter days, *"some shall depart from the faith, giving heed to seducing spirits, and doctrines of devils; speaking lies in hypocrisy; having their conscience seared with a hot iron"* (1 Tim. 4:1-2). These, Jesus said, will be *"gathered and burned in the fire"* (Matt. 13:40).

(Excerpts from *The Harvest*)

Wisdom Versus False Teachings

IN the last days, many who appear to be members of the Body of Christ and sons of God are actually bastards. As children of the devil, these men and women have been seduced by the erroneous doctrines of false teachers and prophets who, according to the apostle Paul, preach "another gospel." (See Second Corinthians 11:4.)

This is true in the church today. Many contemporary doctrines are absolutely contrary to the words of Christ and the teachings of His apostles. These false doctrines emphasize gratifying the lust of the flesh, in contrast to the death that comes through the cross. Their proponents are more concerned with approval and validation of the world, instead of the approval and accreditation of God the Father.

One such false teaching implies that the more material and monetary things you possess, the more spiritually and morally worthwhile you become. They reach this conclusion by reinterpreting Luke 12:15 to read, *"The worth of a man consists in and of the things he possesses,"* replacing the true, literal meaning that says we are to, "Take heed, and beware of covetousness: for a man's life consisteth not in the abundance of the things which he possesseth."

God has given us our measure of faith (see Romans 12:3) to submit to Him, do His will, and further His kingdom here on earth. We are not to use our faith to pursue our own personal agendas and build our own kingdoms.

Like the tares of the field that resemble the wheat, false teachings are usually similar to the truth. Their deceptions are so subtle that many people cannot discern the difference between their hidden lies and the truth.

These false teachings, in most cases, appear to confess Jesus verbally, but they do not submit to Christ's lordship. Centered on selfish ambition and personal agendas, they ignore the will and purpose of God for humankind.

Points to Ponder

False doctrines emphasize gratifying the lust of the flesh.

False doctrines are more concerned with approval and validation of the world, instead of the approval and accreditation of God the Father.

God has given you your measure of faith to submit to Him, do His will, and further His Kingdom here on earth.

Do not to use your faith to pursue your own personal agenda and build your own kingdom.

Learn to discern the difference between their hidden lies and the truth.

Words of Wisdom

Sound doctrine and holy living are the marks of true prophets. Let us remember this. [A] minister's mistakes will not excuse our own.

–J.C. Ryle, *Commentary, Matthew 7*

But there were false prophets also among the people, even as there shall be false teachers among you, who privily shall bring in damnable heresies, even denying the Lord that bought them, and bring upon themselves swift destruction (2 Peter 2:1).

Then, my nursing supervisor praised me one day for my 'deep spirituality.' I thanked her, secretly thrilled my Christian witness had been showing through. My excitement dissolved, though, when I read a book she gave me called *A Course in Miracles.* Although it used Christian lingo like *atonement* and *sanctification,* the concepts were far from Christian. I was puzzled. Weren't we speaking the same language? What had my supervisor meant by *spirituality?*

–Ruth E. Van Reken, "The Truth About Spirituality,"
Christianity Today[1]

Dear friends, do not believe every spirit, but test the spirits to see whether they are from God, because many false prophets have gone out into the world (1 John 4:1 NIV).

MY WISDOM KEYS

36

Wisdom Versus Pride

Pride goes before destruction, a haughty spirit before a fall (Proverbs 16:18 NIV).

Pride comes before a fall. But what is pride? Pride is defined as "being high-minded; showing one's self above others." Another definition states: "Pride is a conceited sense of one's superiority." Pride has caused the fall of many great and gifted individuals.

(Excerpts from *Help Me, I've Fallen and Can't Get Up*)

Wisdom Versus Pride Reflections

THE first known instance of pride occurred before the creation of the earth. Lucifer, the head angel in charge of praise, decided he was going to be greater than God Himself.

> How art thou fallen from Heaven, O Lucifer, son of the morning! how art thou cut down to the ground, which didst weaken the nations! For thou hast said in thine heart, I will ascend into Heaven, I will exalt my throne above the stars of God: I will sit also upon the mount of the congregation, in the sides of the north.... I will be like the most High (Isaiah 14:12-14).

Driven by self-deception, prideful self-delusion, and self-importance, Lucifer considered himself better than God. This explains why most of his statements begin with the word "I."

Lucifer, whose name at one time meant "light-bearer," was cast down by God to earth, where he would be known as satan. No longer a praise leader or a majestic angel, instead he became one who roams to and fro on the earth like a lion looking for someone to devour.

Satan's pride led to his downfall. Pride and selfishness go hand in hand. Usually where there is pride, there is also the prevailing spirit of selfishness. Selfishness is defined as "loving one's self first."

Satan thought he could be better than God Himself. Of course, he was wrong. Satan was deceived. How he even conceived such a thought is beyond imagination. But pride blinds us to the truth and prevents the proud from viewing life realistically.

As we know, satan has never repented. Instead, he tries to deceive as many of God's children as possible and drag them down to share in his dreadful fallen state.

When put into a place of prominence, many of God's children forget who brought them to that place. This arrogant and prideful attitude has caused many to fall from the pinnacle of success and popularity.

Points to Ponder

Pride has caused the fall of many great
and gifted individuals.

Satan's pride led to his downfall.

Pride and selfishness go hand in hand.

Pride blinds you to the truth and prevents the proud from
viewing life realistically.

Satan tries to deceive you and drag you down to share in his
dreadful fallen state.

When put into a place of prominence,
don't forget who brought you to that place.

Words of Wisdom

But after Uzziah became powerful, his pride led to his downfall. He was unfaithful to the Lord his God, and entered the temple of the Lord to burn incense on the altar of incense (2 Chronicles 26:16 NIV).

Those who think too much of themselves don't think enough.

–Amy Carmichael

Pride is that tool of human self-preservation which can be emotion-filled and eventually prove costly. The Bible tells us that a quiet answer turns away anger (see Prov. 15:1); but how then can you possibly win the disagreement? That depends on how you were trained to disagree. Was it loudly and with force or by simply walking away in fear? How would you like to be retrained to deal with those disappointing times of disagreement and anger full of self-preserving pride?

–Steve and Mary Prokopchak, *Called Together*[1]

The focus of health in the soul is humility, while the root of inward corruption is pride. In the spiritual life, nothing stands still. If we are not constantly growing downward into humility, we shall be steadily swelling up and running to seed under the influence of pride.

–J. I. Packer, "Rediscovering Holiness"[2]

God despises pride. Pride usually leads into a terrible fall. Only satan can convince us that we, by our own strength, have accomplished anything good spiritually.

–Curtis C. Thomas, *Practical Wisdom for Pastors*[3]

MY WISDOM KEYS

_____

_____

_____

_____

_____

_____

_____

_____

_____

_____

_____

_____

37

Wisdom of Asking for Help

*There is a way which seemeth right unto a man, but the
end thereof are the ways of death* (Proverbs 14:12).

Are you fighting against God? Maybe you have struggled in
your mind, wondering: Should I ask for help? Who would
be willing to help me? What if they laugh at me? You find
yourself trying to get help from everyone except God.

(Excerpts from *Help Me, I've Fallen and Can't Get Up*)

Wisdom of Asking for Help Reflections

THE apostle Paul, who was formerly named Saul of Tarsus, had persecuted many Christians out of religious zeal. He, too, found it hard to accept the fact that he needed help.

> *And as he journeyed, he came near Damascus: and suddenly there shined round about him a light from Heaven: And he fell to the earth, and heard a voice saying unto him, 'Saul, Saul, why persecutest thou Me?' And he said, 'Who art thou, Lord?' And the Lord said, 'I am Jesus whom thou persecutest: it is hard for thee to kick against the pricks'* (Acts 9:3-5).

What did Jesus mean when he said, "I am Jesus whom thou persecutest: it is hard for thee to kick against the pricks"?

The word *prick* is the King James translation for the word *goad*. Goad means "to sting; a form of aggressive agitation." Today, we say, "He tried to goad me into a fight."

In this passage from Acts, *prick* is used metaphorically to represent the prompting and pricking of the Holy Spirit that God had allowed to come upon Saul's life in an effort to get his attention. The Lord was trying to show Saul that spiritually, he was going down the wrong road and moving in a direction contrary to God's will.

234

Stubborn and hard-headed, Saul insisted on doing things his own way. After all, he was intelligent, capable, religious—and proud of it! As a result, it took a dramatic move of God to knock Saul off his "high horse."

After being blinded by the bright light, this radical zealot found himself in the humble position of needing someone to lead him by the hand. This temporary loss of sight was God's way of showing Saul there was Someone far greater than he.

God was saying, "Saul, why do you kick against the pricks?" In other words, "Why do you fight against what you know is true? Why do you insist on doing things your own way without first consulting Me?"

Is the Lord asking you the same question, "Why do you kick against the pricks?" The American translation puts it this way, "Why do you allow yourself to continue to run into brick walls?"

Points to Ponder

Are you fighting against God?

Are you going down the wrong road and moving in
a direction contrary to God's will?

Do you insist on doing things your own way?

Have you been (or do you need to be)
knocked off your "high horse"?

Are you fighting against yourself and God's will?

Ask Him for help.

Words of Wisdom

If something in your life or body is trying to kill you, if you feel bound up and can't seem to break free, then ask God to kill it before it kills you! When you know your life and destiny are at stake, I urge you to ask God to kill the relationship, the addiction, the unhealthy habit, or the cancer that attacks your body.

–Donald Hilliard, *After the Fall*[1]

I will lift up mine eyes unto the hills, from whence cometh my help (Psalm 121:1).

Whether it be at midnight or six in the morning, God is intently listening for the sound of your voice. He can't wait to hear your praises, worship and prayer requests. If you miss talking with God for a whole day, He misses your voice.

–Linda Sommer, "The Morning Hour," *Charisma Magazine*[2]

As with everything else in life, effective parenting begins with God. Who is better to turn to for the foundational principles of parenting then the Author of life and the Founder of marriage and the family?

–Myles Munroe, *Kingdom Parenting*[3]

MY WISDOM KEYS

38

Wisdom and Rebellion

You may have heard the story about the misbehaving little boy whose mother told him to sit in the corner chair. "I may be sitting on the outside," he said, "but I'm standing on the inside."

That's the way many adults act when they rebel against God. Standing in our own strength, however, puts us most in danger of falling. When we think we are strong, we are easy prey for the devil.

(Excerpt from *Help Me, I've Fallen and Can't Get Up*)

Wisdom and Rebellion Reflections

THE prophet Jonah did not want to do what he knew he was called to do. Instead, he murmured and complained and then tried to run. We can't run from God, but we can run out from the protection of the Lord.

That is what Jonah did, but God didn't stop chasing him. He caused a fish to swallow him.

While in the belly of the great fish, Jonah said, "I've messed up. I've blown it. I've goofed. I've gotten into trouble. I've gotten myself in a mess." Jonah realized he had fallen, and he was now in a place where he had to repent of his rebellion.

Has the devil ever told you, "God is not even thinking about you; God can't see you; God doesn't love you anymore; He doesn't care about you; after all, you sinned"?

In the midst of Jonah's feeble prayer, the thought popped up: "I'm too far gone, and I'm cast out of His sight."

Have you ever had to pray with fear in your heart and uncertainty in your spirit, not knowing in your own mind whether God could hear you or not?

God is not deaf, nor is He hard of hearing. God is not like Grandpa; He's God. He can hear your thoughts afar off. He can hear a snake running through the grass in the middle of a rainstorm. He knows what you are trying to say even before you say it.

God will raise you up if you ask Him. Like Jonah, you don't have to do anything special to get God's attention. All He asks is that you humble yourself. God wants you to be delivered out of your desperate situation, but it is up to you not to resist the Holy Ghost. Submit humbly to God; resist the devil and the devil will flee from you. First, you must submit—as Jonah did—to God and His will for your life.

Points to Ponder

Standing in your own strength puts you in danger of falling.

When you think you're strong,
you are easy prey for the devil.

You can't run from God, but you can run out from
under the protection of the Lord.

God can hear your thoughts afar off.

Humble yourself.

Resist the devil, and the devil will flee from you.

Words of Wisdom

How could a loving God send sinners to hell? He doesn't. They volunteer.

⟨ ⟩

Once there, they don't want to leave. The hearts of damned fools never soften; their minds never change. '*Men were scorched with great heat, and they blasphemed the name of God who has power over these plagues; and they did not repent and give Him glory'* (Rev. 16:9 NKJV). Contrary to the idea that hell prompts remorse, it doesn't. It intensifies blasphemy.

–Max Lucado, *Every Knee Shall Bow*[1]

⟨ ⟩

My friend, I know that like me, you want the great blessing that comes from a love relationship with our heavenly Father to be visited upon your life. The Bible contains very clear guidelines on how we can experience the blessings promised to God's children—and I want so much for you to understand them and make them a reality in your life. Are you ready to apply God's principles and begin your journey of blessings as His child?

–Benny Hinn, *God Is Always on Time*[2]

⟨ ⟩

For rebellion is as the sin of witchcraft, and stubbornness is as iniquity and idolatry. Because thou hast rejected the word of the Lord, He hath also rejected thee (1 Samuel 15:23).

⟨ ⟩

What are we? We are rebels made in God's image in need of redemption that only Christ has provided. Yes, we have the capacity for greatness, but also the capacity for wretchedness. The solution to the human puzzle is found not in secular humanism or other philosophies that remove God from the picture, but, rather, the solution is found in God's Word.

–Robert Velarde, *Rebels Against God*[3]

MY WISDOM KEYS

39

Wisdom and Superman

The best parts of school when I was an eight-year-old were recess and the walk home from school. I liked recess because it gave me an opportunity to stretch my legs and play with my friends. I liked the walk home from school because I usually had a quarter buried deep within my pocket, hidden somewhere beneath the bubble gum, the baseball cards, and all the other paraphernalia that eight-year-olds think are valuable.

(Excerpts from *It's Time to Reveal What God Longs to Heal*)

Wisdom and Superman Reflections

THAT quarter of mine was saved for the brightly colored books that were stacked in a display for all the children to see. There were all of my old friends—Superman and Captain Marvel, Captain America and Spiderman. I would purchase a copy of the latest issue and hurry a little farther down Troy Road. Once I found the old path that led up the hill behind the house, I would start my ascent to the big rock beneath the apple tree. There, hidden from public scrutiny, I would pull out my prized hero magazine and imagine that I was one of these men, a superhero who could transform as needed into anything necessary to destroy the villain.

We need heroes today. We need someone to believe in and look up to. We need someone who has accomplished something to give us the courage to believe in the invisible and feel the intangible. We need role models and men whose shadows we may stand in, men who provide a cool refreshing place of safety away from the despair of our oppressive society. It's just that all the "supermen" in the Church seem to have somehow gotten zapped by "kryptonite." Either they or their reputations have wilted into the abyss of human failure.

What are we going to do as we face this generation? From drug-using political officials to prostitute-purchasing preachers, the stars are falling on the heads of this generation! All of their wonder and dreams have turned into a comic book—a comic book that somehow doesn't seem funny anymore. Where did the heroes go?

This isn't just a church issue. We're suffering from an eroding sense of family, not just of family values. The entire concept of the family, period, has been crumbling because of this society's growing acceptance of non-traditional families. More and more women have chosen to be mothers without choosing fathers, while others have become single parents by necessity, not by choice. The gay community has added to the confusion by establishing "homes" that do not reflect God's original plan for child-rearing. So now we have twisted homes that are producing twisted children.

Points to Ponder

You need someone to believe in and look up to.

You need someone who has accomplished something.

You need someone to give you the courage to believe in the
invisible and feel the intangible.

Have your wonder and dreams turned into a comic book?

Are you suffering from an eroding sense of family,
not just of family values?

God is the ultimate Superhero.

Words of Wisdom

Here are only a few of the "super" men and women of the Christian faith:[1]

- F. F. Bosworth—One of the first healing evangelists; wrote the best-seller *Christ the Healer*

- David Brainerd—Among the first to teach North American Indians the Gospel of Christ

- John Bunyan—Wrote *Pilgrim's Progress*

- Mildred Cable—Missionary to China, obedient to God's call; spread the Gospel in the Gobi Desert

- John Calvin—Christian reformer

- Amy Carmichael—Missionary to India

- Jonathan Edwards—Revival preacher

- Billy Graham—The people's evangelist; "Hour of Decision"

- John Knox—Reformation in Scotland

- David Livingstone—World-famous missionary from Scotland who took God's light to Africa

- Martin Luther—Father of Reformation

- John Newton—Christian opposed to the slave trade

- Corrie Ten Boom—Heroic saint and evangelist

- John and Charles Wesley—Methodist founders

- William Wilberforce—English Christian who brought slavery to an end
- John Wycliffe—Translated first Bible to English

MY WISDOM KEYS

_____

_____

_____

_____

_____

_____

_____

_____

_____

_____

_____

_____

40

Wisdom to Celebrate!

Have you allowed God to stand in the bow of your ship and speak peace to the thing that once terrified you? We can only benefit from resolved issues. The great tragedy is that most of us keep our pain active. Consequently, our power is never activated because our past remains unresolved. If we want to see God's power come from the pain of an experience, we must allow the process of healing to take us far beyond bitterness into a resolution that releases us from the prison and sets us free.

(Excerpts from *It's Time to Reveal What God Longs to Heal*)

Wisdom to Celebrate! Reflections

GOD'S healing process makes us free to taste life again, free to trust again, and free to live without the restrictive force of threatening fears. Someone may say, "I don't want to trust again." That is only because you are not healed. To never trust again is to live on the pinnacle of a tower. You are safe from life's threatening grasp, but you are so detached from life that you soon lose consciousness of people, places, dates, and events. You become locked into a time warp. You always talk about the past because you stopped living years ago. Listen to your speech. You discuss the past as if it were the present because the past has stolen the present right out of your hand! In the name of Jesus, get it back!

Celebration is in order. Yes, it is time to celebrate—regardless of whether you've lost a marriage, a partnership, or a personal friend. Celebration is in order because you were split from your Siamese twin and you are not dead. You are still alive! (Or at least you will be the moment you decide to be.) Are you ready to live, or do you still need to subject all your friends to a history class? Will you continue your incessant raging and blubbering about that which no one can change—the past?

Step into the present. Your friends will celebrate—and so will your own mind! It has been locked down, tightly tied to dead issues, and it wants to be creative and inspired again! Could it be possible that there are still those around you who

256

want to be a part of your life, now that you have chosen to stop dwelling among the dead and in the tombs?

Perhaps I have been hard on you, but I am only trying to jump-start your heart and put you back into the presence of a real experience, far from the dank, dark valley of regret and remorse. It is easy to unconsciously live in a euphoric, almost historical mirage that causes current opportunities to evade you.

The time to celebrate is now!

Points to Ponder

God's healing process makes you free to taste life.

God's healing process makes you free to trust again.

God's healing process allows you
to live without threatening fears.

Stop dwelling among the dead and in the tombs.

Step into the present.

Live to celebrate!

Words of Wisdom

This is what the New Covenant meal is all about. When we partake of it, we are not just remembering a life given; we are celebrating a life received. It is God's life, and we have received it.

–Dr. Richard Booker, *The Miracle of the Scarlet Thread*[1]

'For this son of mine was dead and is alive again; he was lost and is found.' So they began to celebrate (Luke 15:24 NIV).

God is not a cosmic killjoy. I know some people who believe He is. They think God runs around saying, 'There's one having fun; get him!' They believe God wants to rain on everybody's parade. But that isn't so. God made you. He knows how you operate best. And He knows what makes you happy. The happiness He gives doesn't stop when the party's over. It lasts because it comes from deep within.

–John MacArthur, *You Can Trust the Bible*[2]

King David was able to celebrate and have a great feast after his first son with Bathsheba died as a result of God's judgment. David's servants were very surprised by his behavior because they had seen him mourn with fasting over his ailing son, and he had refused to eat while his boy was fighting for his life. But as soon as they told King David that his baby boy had actually died, he stopped mourning, washed himself, and then called for a huge feast. If he had acted on his external circumstances, he would have stayed in sorrow.

–Jacqueline McCullough, *Satisfaction of the Soul*[3]

My Wisdom Keys

_____

_____

_____

_____

_____

_____

_____

_____

_____

_____

_____

_____

_____

Endnotes

Note: Short quotes are taken from Grace Quotes; http://www.thegracetabernacle.org/quotes/grace_qs_bkgrnd.html; accessed 7/10-14/09.

Chapter 1

1. *Myles Munroe Devotional & Journal* (Shippensburg, PA: Destiny Image Publishers, 2007), Week 18, Day 5.

Chapter 2

1. Joyce Meyer, *Knowing God Intimately* (New York: Warner Faith, 2003), 21.

2. Don Nori Sr., *Manifest Presence* (Shippensburg, PA: Destiny Image Publishers, 2009), 124.

Chapter 3

1. Kim Clement, *Call Me Crazy, But I'm Hearing God* (Shippensburg, PA: Destiny Image Publishers, 2007), 22-23.

2. Sid Roth, *They Thought for Themselves* (Brunswick, GA: M V Press, 1999).

3. Mark Virkler, http://www.cwgministries.org/Four-Keys-to-Hearing-Gods-Voice.htm; accessed 7/10/09.

Chapter 4

1. Bill Johnson, *Strengthen Yourself in the Lord* (Shippensburg, PA: Destiny Image Publishers, 2007), 13.

2. Norman Vincent Peale, *The Power of Positive Thinking* (New York: Ballantine Books, 1996), 166.

Chapter 5

1. Rick Warren, *The Purpose Driven Life* (Grand Rapids, MI: Zondervan, 2007), 11.

2. Marie Chapian, *Angels in Our Lives* (Shippensburg, PA: Destiny Image Publishers, 2006).

3. Bob Lenz, *Grace* (Shippensburg, PA: Destiny Image Publishers, 2008), 114.

Chapter 6

1. Faisal Malick, *Positioned to Bless* (Shippensburg, PA: Destiny Image Publishers, 2008), 92-93.

2. Billy Joe Daugherty, *Knocked Down, But Not Out* (Shippensburg, PA: Destiny Image Publishers, 2006), 83.

Chapter 7

1. Noel Jones, *God's Gonna Make You Laugh* (Shippensburg, PA: Destiny Image Publishers, 2007), 115.

2. John Milton, *Paradise Regained* (Shippensburg, PA: Destiny Image Publishers, 2007), 92.

Chapter 8

1. Flo Ellers, *Activating the Angelic* (Shippensburg, PA: Destiny Image Publishers, 2008), 89.

2. John Crowder, *The New Mystics* (Shippensburg, PA: Destiny Image Publishers, 2006), 287.

Chapter 9

1. Israel Kim, *Find Your Promised Land* (Shippensburg, PA: Destiny Image Publishers, 2009), 71.

Chapter 10

1. Frank Bailey, *Holy Spirit, The Promised One* (Shippensburg, PA: Destiny Image Publishers, 1998), 55.

2. Bruce Allen, *Promise of the Third Day* (Shippensburg, PA: Destiny Image Publishers, 2007), 150-151.

3. Benedict Carey, "A Neuroscientific Look at Speaking in Tongues," *New York Times,* November 7, 2006.

Chapter 11

1. Larry Kreider and Dennis De Grasse, *Supernatural Living* (Shippensburg, PA: Destiny Image Publishers, 2009), 35.

2. Frank Bailey, *Holy Spirit, The Promised One* (Shippensburg, PA: Destiny Image Publishers, 1998), 89.

3. Kris Vallotton, *Developing a Supernatural Lifestyle* (Shippensburg, PA: Destiny Image Publishers, 2007), 166.

Chapter 12

1. Kris Den Besten, *Shine: Five Empowering Principles for a Rewarding Life* (Shippensburg, PA: Destiny Image Publishers, 2008), 110.

2. Mark Van Deman, *A Traveler's Guide to the Spirit Realm* (Shippensburg, PA: Destiny Image Publishers, 2008), 83.

3. James W. Goll and Lou Engle, *The Call of the Elijah Revolution* (Shippensburg, PA: Destiny Image Publishers, 2008), 60-61.

Chapter 13

1. Don Nori Sr., *The Love Shack* (Shippensburg, PA: Destiny Image Publishers, 2009), 38.

2. Dr. Richard Booker, *Living in His Presence* (Shippensburg, PA: Destiny Image Publishers, 1986), 49.

Chapter 14

1. Derek Prince, *Faith to Live By* (New Kensington, PA: Whitaker House, 1977), 48-49.

2. Alan Vincent, *The Good Fight of Faith* (Shippensburg, PA: Destiny Image Publishers, 2008), 102.

Chapter 15

1. Don Nori Sr., *Secrets of the Most Holy Place Volume Two* (Shippensburg, PA: Destiny Image Publishers, 2004), 46.

2. Sid Roth, *The Incomplete Church* (Shippensburg, PA: Destiny Image Publishers, 2007), 32.

Chapter 16

1. Morris Cerullo, *How to Pray* (Shippensburg, PA: Destiny Image Publishers, 2004), 71.

2. Neil T. Anderson, *Praying by the Power of the Spirit* (Eugene, OR: Harvest House, 2003), 10.

Chapter 17

1. Greg Holmes, *If He Builds It, They Will Come* (Shippensburg, PA: Destiny Image Publishers, 2007), 118.

2. Marion Meyers, *The ABC's of Emotions* (Shippensburg, PA: Destiny Image Publishers, 2006), 84.

3. Jerry Bridges, *The Practice of Godliness* (Colorado Springs, CO: NavPress, 1996), 179.

Chapter 18

1. Bill Wilson, *Christianity in the Crosshairs* (Shippensburg, PA: Destiny Image Publishers, 2004), 78.

2. Robert D. Jones, *Bad Memories: Getting Past Your Past* (Phillipsburg, NJ: P&R Publishing, 2004).

Chapter 19

1. Tom Wells, *A Vision for Missions* (Carlisle, PA: The Banner of Truth Trust), 84.

2. Doug Stringer, *Hope for a Fatherless Generation* (Shippensburg, PA: Destiny Image Publishers, 2009), 85.

3. Dan Doriani, *The Life of a God-Made Man* (Wheaton, IL: Crossway, 2001), 150.

Chapter 20

1. Leigh Valentine, *Successfully You!* (Shippensburg, PA: Destiny Image Publishers, 2008), 154.

2. Charles R. Swindoll, *Christian Reader,* v. 33, n. 4.

3. Reggie White, *Broken Promises, Blinded Dreams* (Shippensburg, PA: Destiny Image Publishers, 2003), 41.

Chapter 21

1. Carl Hampsch, *Opposites Attract* (Shippensburg, PA: Destiny Image Publishers, 2007), 109.

Chapter 22

1. Steve Shultz, *Can't You Talk Louder God?* (Shippensburg, PA: Destiny Image Publishers, 2007), 26.

2. Wes Roberts and Glenn C. Marshall, *Reclaiming God's Original Intent for the Church* (Colorado Springs: NavPress, 2004), 18.

3. John MacArthur, *The Master's Plan for the Church* (Chicago: Moody, 1991), 159.

Chapter 23

1. Joyce Meyer Ministries; http://www.joycemeyer.org/OurMinistries/EverydayAnswers.

Chapter 24

1. Elmer L. Towns, *Praying the Gospels* (Shippensburg, PA: Destiny Image, 2007), 153.

2. Jerry Bridges, *Trusting God* (Colorado Springs: NavPress, 1988), 188.

ENDNOTES

Chapter 25

1. Noel Jones and Scott Chaplan, *Vow of Prosperity* (Shippensburg, PA: Destiny Image, 2007), 30.

2. Donald Whitney, *Spiritual Disciplines for the Christian Life* (Colorado Springs: NavPress, 1991), 238.

3. Joyce Meyer, *The Root of Rejection* (Nashville, TN: FaithWords, 2002), 8.

Chapter 26

1. James W. Goll and Julia Loren, *Shifting Shadows of Supernatural Experience* (Shippensburg, PA: Destiny Image, 2007), 136.

2. Cal Thomas, "The Authority of the State," *Tabletalk*, March 2009, 21.

3. Madame Jeanne-Marie Bouvier de la Motte-Guyon, *Autobiography of Madam Guyon. (Valdebooks), 209, Chapter 8.*

Chapter 27

1. Don Nori Sr., *Manifest Presence* (Shippensburg, PA: Destiny Image, 2009), 20.

2. Dr. Francis J. Sizer, *Into His Presence* (Shippensburg, PA: Destiny Image, 2009), 148.

3. Robert Stearns, *Prepare the Way (or Get Out of the Way!)* (Shippensburg, PA: Destiny Image, 1999), 41.

Chapter 28

1. John Bunyan (ed. Jim Pappas Jr.), *Pilgrim's Progress, Part 2 Christiana* (Shippensburg, PA: Destiny Image, 2005), 109-110.

2. Faisal Malick, *The Destiny of Islam in the Endtimes* (Shippensburg, PA: Destiny Image, 2007), 31.

3. Nancy Leigh DeMoss, *A Place of Quiet Rest* (Chicago: Moody, 2000), 235.

Chapter 29

1. Dr. Lynn Hiles, *The Revelation of Jesus Christ* (Shippensburg, PA: Destiny Image, 2007), 170.

2. Fred and Sharon Wright, *The World's Greatest Revivals* (Shippensburg, PA: Destiny Image, 2007), 202

Chapter 30

1. Myles Munroe, *The Purpose and Power of Praise and Worship* (Shippensburg, PA: Destiny Image, 2000).

2. Mark A. Brewer, *What's Your Spiritual Quotient?* (Shippensburg, PA: Destiny Image, 2008).

3. CBN.com; 700 Club; "Keys to Powerful Living: Praise"; http://www.cbn.com/spirituallife/cbnTeachingSheets/keys-Praise.aspx; accessed 7/13/09.

Chapter 31

1. SonicFlood, "Lord, I Lift Your Name on High," 2001Gotee Records.

2. Elmer Towns, *Praying the Book of Acts* (Shippensburg, PA: Destiny Image, 2007), 25.

3. Michael W. Smith, recording artist, "Smitty Takes a Stand," http://www.christianitytoday.com/music/artists/michaelwsmith/michaelwsmith.html; accessed 7/13/09.

Chapter 32

1. John MacArthur, *The Ultimate Priority* (Chicago: Moody Press 1983), 13.

Chapter 33

1. James Wilson, *Living as Ambassadors of Relationships* (Shippensburg, PA: Destiny Image, 2008), 141.

Chapter 34

1. Derek Knoke, *God in MySpace* (Shippensburg, PA: Destiny Image, 2008), 45.

Chapter 35

1. Ruth E. Van Reken, "The Truth About Spirituality," *Christianity Today;* http://www.christianitytoday.com/tcw/1996/novdec/6w6050.html; accessed 7/14/09.

Chapter 36

1. Steve and Mary Prokopchak, *Called Together* (Shippensburg, PA: Destiny Image, 2009).

2. J.I. Packer, "Rediscovering Holiness" *Christianity Today*, v. 36, n. 13.

3. Curtis C. Thomas, *Practical Wisdom for Pastors* (Wheaton, IL: Crossway Books, 2001), 209.

Chapter 37

1. Donald Hilliard, *After the Fall* (Shippensburg, PA: Destiny Image, 2007), 95.

2. Linda Sommer, "The Morning Hour," Charisma Magazine; http://www.charismamag.com/index.php/newsletters/daily-

devotionals/around-the-word-in-365-days/22486-the-morning-hour; accessed 7/14/09.

3. Myles Munroe and David Burrows, *Kingdom Parenting* (Shippensburg, PA: Destiny Image, 2007), 9.

Chapter 38

1. Max Lucado, "Every Knee Shall Bow"; http://www.maxlucado.com/email/2008/03.20.html; accessed 7/14/09.

2. Benny Hinn, "God Is Always on Time"; http://www.bennyhinn.org/articles/articledesc.cfm?id=3036; accessed 7/14/09.

3. Robert Velarde, "Rebels Against God"; Focus on the Family.com; http://www.focusonthefamily.com/faith/the_study_of_god/why_study_god/rebels_against_god.aspx; accessed 7/14/09.

Chapter 39

1. Christian Heroes.com; http://www.christianheroes.com/index/christian_heroes_people.asp; accessed 7/14/09.

Chapter 40

1. Dr. Richard Booker, *The Miracle of the Scarlet Thread* (Shippensburg, PA: Destiny Image, 2008), 202.

2. John MacArthur, *You Can Trust the Bible* (Chicago: Moody Press, 1988), 19-20.

3. Jacqueline McCullough, *Satisfaction of the Soul* (Shippensburg, PA: Destiny Image, 2007).

88983791R00163

Made in the USA
Middletown, DE
13 September 2018